Table of Contents

Name: Luke

My Story

Directions: Fill in the blanks. Use these sentences to write a story about yourself.

I feel happy when ______________________________.

I feel sad when ______________________________.

I am good at ______________________________.

Words that describe me: ______________ ______________

______________ ______________ ______________.

I can help at home by ______________________________.

My friends like me because ______________________________.

I like to ______________________________.

My favorite food is ______________________________.

My favorite animal is ______________________________.

Now . . . take your answers and write a story about **you**!

Name: ______________________________

Word Configurations

Directions: Match the figures to the words below.

Example:

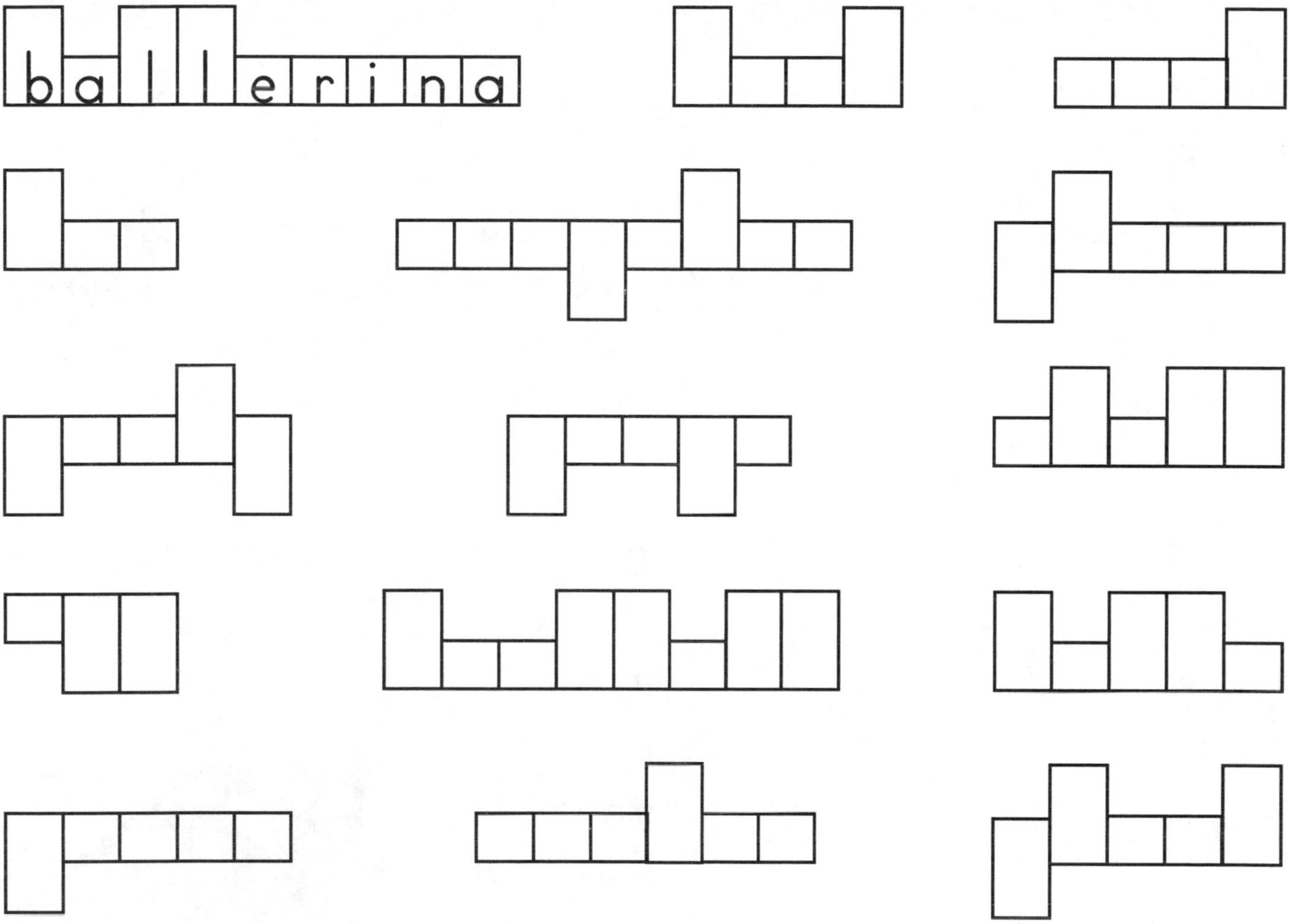

b a l l e r i n a

ballerina	computer	shelf
egg	cactus	party
book	table	grape
piano	box	wood
football	plant	glass

Name: ____________________

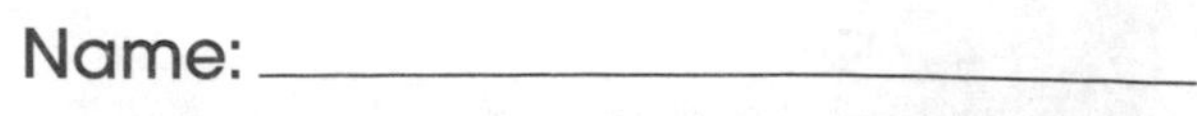

Phonics

Some words are more difficult to read because they have one or more silent letters. Many words you already know are like this.

Examples: wrong and **night**.

Directions: Circle the silent letters in each word. The first one is done for you.

(w)rong	answer	autumn	whole
knife	hour	wrap	comb
sigh	straight	knee	known
lamb	taught	scent	daughter
whistle	wrote	knew	crumb

Directions: Draw a line between the rhyming words. The first one is done for you.

knew	try
sees	bowl
taut	stone
wrote	true
comb	song
straight	trees
sigh	home
known	great
wrong	caught
whole	boat

Name: ____________________

Phonics

Sometimes letters make sounds you don't expect. Two consonants can work together to make the sound of one consonant. The **f** sound can be made by **ph**, as in the word **elephant**. The consonants **gh** are most often silent, as in the words **night** and **though**. But they also can make the **f** sound as in the word **laugh**.

Directions: Circle the letters that make the **f** sound. Write the correct word from the box to complete each sentence.

ele(ph)ant	cough	laugh	telephone	phonics
dolphins	enough	tough	alphabet	rough

1. The **dolphins** were playing in the sea.
2. Did you have ____________ time to do your homework?
3. A cold can make you ____________ and sneeze.
4. The ____________ ate peanuts with his trunk.
5. The road to my school is ____________ and bumpy.
6. You had a ____________ call this morning.
7. The ____________ meat was hard to chew.
8. Studying ____________ will help you read better.
9. The ____________ has 26 letters in it.
10. We began to ____________ when the clowns came in.

Name: ______________________

Phonics

There are several consonants that make the **k** sound: **c** when followed by a, o or u as in **cow** or **cup**; the letter **k** as in **milk**; the letters **ch** as in **Christmas** and **ck** as in **black**.

Directions: Read the following words. Circle the letters that make the **k** sound. The first one is done for you.

a(ch)e	school	market	comb
camera	deck	darkness	Christmas
necklace	doctor	stomach	crack
nickel	skin	thick	escape

Directions: Use your own words to finish the following sentences. Use words with the **k** sound.

1. If I had a nickel, I would ______________________.

2. My doctor is very ______________________.

3. We bought ripe, juicy tomatoes at the ______________________.

4. If I had a camera now,
   I would take a picture of ______________________.

5. When my stomach aches, ______________________.

Name: ____________________

Phonics

The **sh** sound is usually made by the letters **sh**. Sometimes it is made by the letters **ci** as in **musician**, **si** as in **possession** or **ti** as in **station**.

Directions: Read the following words. Circle the letters that make the **sh** sound.

wash	nation	delicious
action	rush	shine
special	attention	vacation

permission

Directions: Use the word box above to find the words hidden in the puzzle below. One is done for you.

i	n	s	u	t	e	r	u	s	r	t
t	w	d	e	l	i	c	i	o	u	s
v	a	c	a	t	i	o	n	i	s	h
c	s	p	e	c	i	a	l	a	h	i
a	h	t	i	o	n	t	i	c	i	n
a	c	t	i	o	n	s	h	t	i	e
s	u	r	t	n	a	t	i	o	n	s
t	p	e	r	m	i	s	s	i	o	n
s	a	t	t	e	n	t	i	o	n	h

Phonics Story

Directions: Read the story. Underline the words with silent letters. Circle the words with the **k** sound. Put a box around the words with letters that make the **sh** sound. Answer the question at the end of the story.

Stephanie, the elephant, was having a rough time with a bad cough. Stephanie's mother was quite worried about her daughter. She got right on the telephone to the doctor. He rushed over to find out what was wrong with the thick-skinned, but very sick, creature.

The doctor took one look at Stephanie's green skin and took quick action. He wrote out a prescription for Stephanie's queasy stomach, and Stephanie's mother made her special alphabet soup.

Before she knew it, Stephanie's aches were quite gone, and Stephanie was a happy and healthy elephant, laughing and playing once again.

What do you do when you get sick?

____

____

____

Name: ____________________

Phonics

In some word "families," the vowels have a long sound when you would expect them to have a short sound. For example, the **i** has a short sound in **chill**, but a long sound in **child**. The **o** has a short sound in **cost**, but a long sound in **most**.

Directions: Read the words in the word box below. Write the words that have a long vowel sound under the word **LONG**, and the words that have a short vowel sound under the word **SHORT**. (Remember, a long vowel says its name—like **a** in **ate**.)

old	odd	gosh	gold	sold	soft	toast	frost	lost	most
doll	roll	bone	done	kin	mill	mild	wild	blink	blind

LONG		SHORT	
bone	________	doll	________
________	________	________	________
________	________	________	________
________	________	________	________
________	________	________	________

Name: ____________________

Phonics Riddle

Directions: Use the key to match the number with the letter. Write the riddle and the answer.

___ ___ ___ ___   ___ ___   ___ ___ ___
23 8 1 20   4 15   25 15 21

___ ___ ___ ___   ___   ___ ___ ___ ___ ___ ___
3 1 12 12   1   18 1 2 2 9 20

___ ___ ___ ___   ___ ___ ___ ___ ___?
23 9 20 8   6 12 5 1 19

Answer:

___ ___ ___ ___   ___ ___ ___ ___ ___!
2 21 7 19   2 21 14 14 25

Ha-ha-ha!

Ha-ha-ha!

Key

A	B	C	D	E	F	G	H	I	J	K	L	M
1	2	3	4	5	6	7	8	9	10	11	12	13
N	**O**	**P**	**Q**	**R**	**S**	**T**	**U**	**V**	**W**	**X**	**Y**	**Z**
14	15	16	17	18	19	20	21	22	23	24	25	26

Name: ______________________

Vowel Bingo

Directions: Cut out the arrow and spinner on this page and glue them onto cardboard. Use a paper clip or paper fastener to attach the arrow to the spinner. Cut out the bingo boards on the next page. Use beans or cereal as markers. Players take turns spinning and covering words on their game boards with the vowel sound shown on the spinner. The first player to cover five in a row, either vertically (up and down), horizontally (sideways) or diagonally (corner to corner) wins the game!

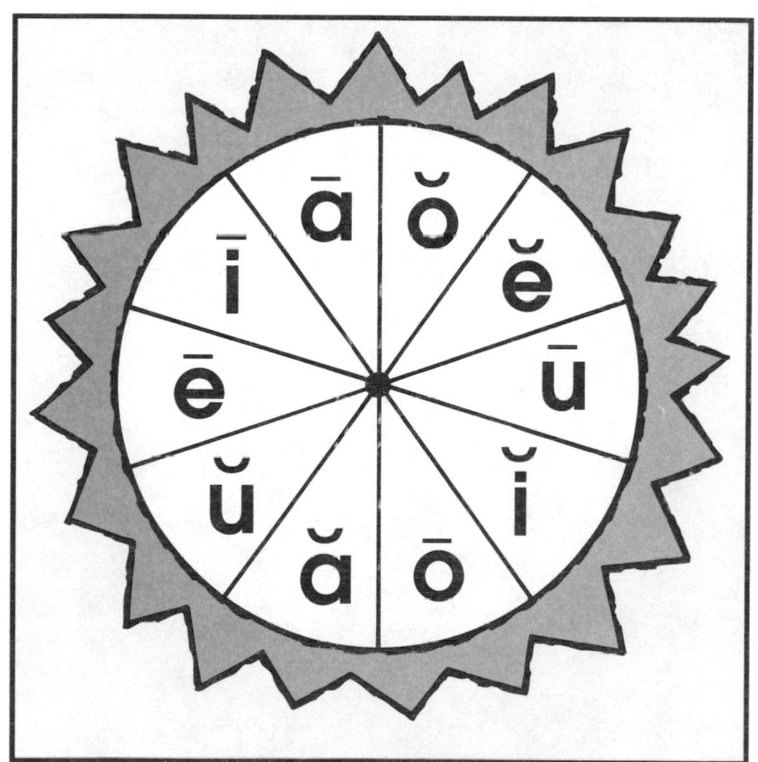

˘ Represents Short Vowel Sounds

¯ Represents Long Vowel Sounds

Vowel Bingo Spinner

THE VOWELS:

a e i o u

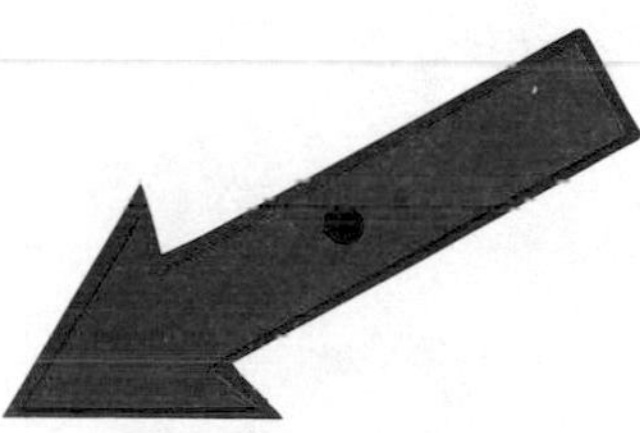

Page is blank for cutting exercise on previous page.

Name: ____________________

cut ✂

Vowel Bingo

cat	ache	icicle	bus	sleeper
sprinkle	bike	tube	hope	apple
stapler	poke	FREE	soap	cutter
beach	pickle	reuse	let	petted
splat	opposite	villain	otter	huge

cut ✂

Vowel Bingo

boat	fuse	crib	clock	cub
egg	make	butter	track	feet
treat	trip	FREE	hay	octopus
perfume	spoke	mice	grind	pillow
rack	matter	setting	cube	choke

Page is blank for cutting exercise on previous page.

Name: ______________________

Phonics

Sometimes, vowels have unusual sounds that are neither short nor long. For example, often when an **a** is followed by an **l**, instead of the short **a** sound, as in **apple**, it has the sound in **ball**. Sometimes an **o** has the sound of short **u**, as in **done**.

Directions: Read the words in the following word "families." Write another word in each group.

The **al** and **all** families:
also, always, ball, small, tall, ______________________

The **alk** family:
chalk, stalk, talk, ______________________

The **alt** family:
halt, malt, ______________________

The **o** family:
done, come, other, ______________________

Directions: Draw lines to match the rhyming words.

glove	call
pull	halt
wall	shove
salt	talk
walk	full

Name: ______________________

Syllables

All words can be divided into **syllables**. Syllables are word parts which have one vowel sound in each part.

Directions: Draw a line between the syllable part and write the word on the correct line below. The first one is done for you.

lit|tle	bumblebee	pillow
truck	dazzle	dog
pencil	flag	angelic
rejoicing	ant	telephone

1 SYLLABLE	2 SYLLABLES	3 SYLLABLES
______	little	______
______	______	______
______	______	______
______	______	______

Name: ______________________

Syllables

When the letters **le** come at the end of a word, they sometimes have the sound of **ul**, as in raffle.

Directions: Draw a line to match the syllables so they make words. The first one is done for you.

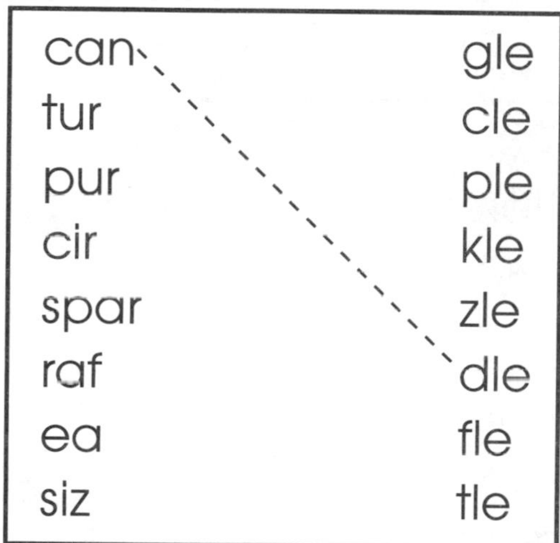

can	gle
tur	cle
pur	ple
cir	kle
spar	zle
raf	dle
ea	fle
siz	tle

Directions: Use the words you made to complete the sentences. One is done for you.

1. Will you buy a ticket for our school <u>raffle</u>?
2. The ____________________ pulled his head into his shell.
3. We could hear the bacon ____________________ in the pan.
4. The baby had one ____________________ on her birthday cake.
5. My favorite color is ____________________.
6. Look at that diamond ____________________!
7. The bald ____________________ is our national bird.
8. Draw a ____________________ around the correct answer.

Name: ______________________

Review

Directions: Use words from the word box to fill in each blank. Each word is used only once. There is an example for each one.

knob	black	rush	laugh	bold	people
needle	school	host	autumn	delicious	handle
dolphin	most	quick	action	night	elephant

1. Write three words with silent letters from the word box:

   comb, ______________, ______________, ______________

2. Write three words with the f sound:

   alphabet, ______________, ______________, ______________

3. Write three words with the k sound:

   camp, ______________, ______________, ______________

4. Write three words with the sh sound:

   nation, ______________, ______________, ______________

5. Write three words with the long o sound:

   gold, ______________, ______________, ______________

6. Write three words in which le has the sound of ul:

   purple, ______________, ______________, ______________

Name: ____________________

Riddle

Directions: Use the key to match the number with the letter. Write the riddle and the answer.

__ __ __   __ __   __ __ __
8 15 23   4 15   25 15 21

__ __ __ __ __   __
19 20 1 18 20   1

__ __ __ __ __ __ __   __ __ __ __?
6 9 18 5 6 12 25   18 1 3 5

Answer:

__ __   __ __ __ __   __ __ __ __,
15 14   25 15 21 18   13 1 18 11

__ __ __,   __ __ __ __!
19 5 20   7 12 15 23

HA-HA-HA!

Key

A	B	C	D	E	F	G	H	I	J	K	L	M
1	2	3	4	5	6	7	8	9	10	11	12	13
N	O	P	Q	R	S	T	U	V	W	X	Y	Z
14	15	16	17	18	19	20	21	22	23	24	25	26

Name: ______________________

Vocabulary

Directions: Find each word in the word box and circle it. The first one is done for you.

Word box							
canoe	t	c	a	n	h	s	p
chains	c	a	n	o	e	t	i
spider	h	s	o	n	s	c	r
star	a	t	i	s	t	h	e
tear	i	c	s	h	a	i	s
noise	n	t	e	a	r	n	t
chin	s	p	i	d	e	r	g

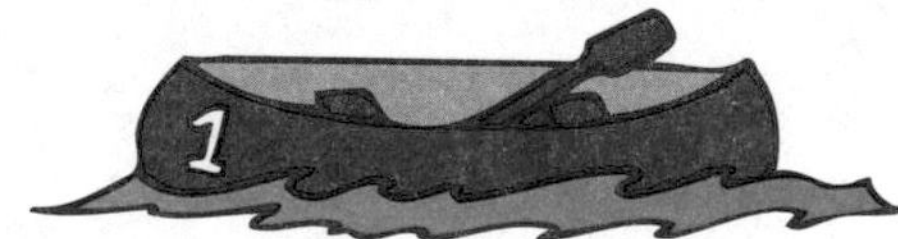

Directions: Write the correct word from the word box to finish each sentence.

1. I have to sew up a ______________________ in my shirt.
2. It is fun to make a wish on a ______________________.
3. There was a ______________________'s web over the door.
4. Our porch swing is held up by ______________________.
5. We paddled a ______________________ down the river.
6. A lawn mower makes a lot of ______________________.
7. I fell down and cut my ______________________.

Name: ____________________

Transportation Vocabulary

Directions: Unscramble the words to spell the names of kinds of transportation. The first one is done for you.

behelwworar — wheel b a r r o w

anirt — t _ _ _ n

moobattor — moto _ _ _ _ t

crattor — t _ _ c _ _ _

ceicbly — b _ _ _ _ _ e

tocker — r _ _ _ _ t

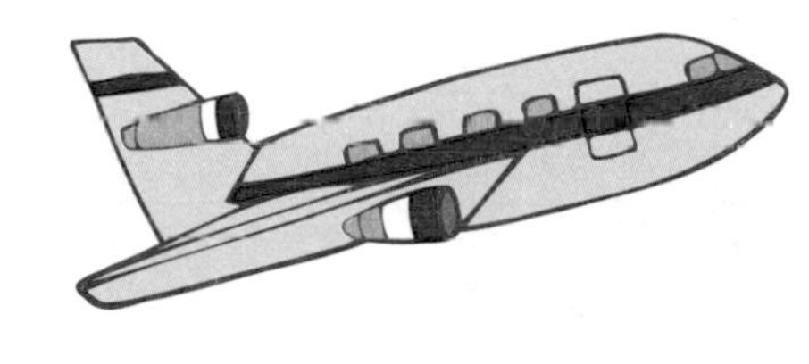

etobimuloa — aut _ _ _ _ _ _ e

rilanape — a _ _ p _ _ _ e

Directions: Use a word from above to complete each sentence.

1. My mother uses a ____________ to move dirt to her garden.
2. The __________ blasted the spaceship off the launching pad.
3. We flew on an ____________ to visit my aunt in Florida.
4. My grandfather drives a very old ____________.
5. We borrowed Fred's ____________ to go water skiing.
6. You should always look both ways when crossing a ____________ track.
7. I hope I get a new ____________ for my birthday.

Name: ____________________

Cooking Tools Vocabulary

Directions: Unscramble the words to spell the names of things you use when you cook. The first one is done for you.

miwrcovae microwave

easmriugn spuc ____________________

imrxe ____________________

stop ____________________

pnas ____________________

ponoss ____________________

veon ____________________

mrtie ____________________

tsla nad pppeer ____________________

wlbos ____________________

What is your favorite recipe?

____

Name: ____________________

Vocabulary

Directions: Use the word box to find the hidden words in the puzzle below.

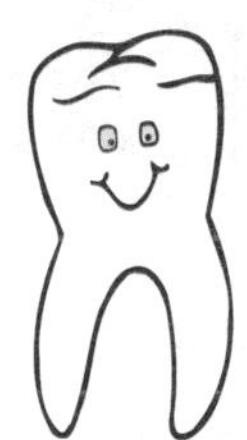

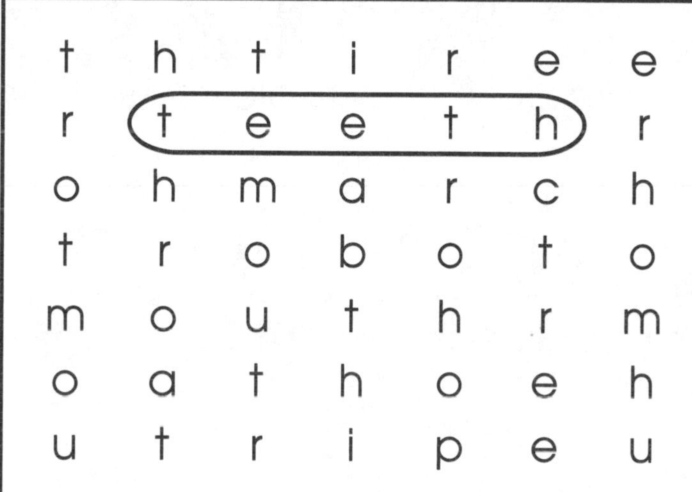

teeth	throat	mouth	robot	tree
trot	tire	March	trip	

Directions: Use a word from the word box to complete each sentence.

1. It is hard to swallow when you have a sore ____________________.
2. Can a ____________________ do your chores for you?
3. The first day of spring is in ____________________.
4. Be careful not to ____________________ over that toy on the floor.
5. A dentist takes care of your ____________________.
6. Our cat was stuck up in a ____________________.
7. Our horse likes to ____________________ around the track.
8. The car has a flat ____________________.

Name: ______________________

Career Vocabulary

Directions: Read the sentences, then follow the directions.

Doctors have many years of schooling. They must learn all about how the human body works. Their training helps them figure out why people are sick or hurt and how to help them.

Astronauts are trained to fly spaceships and to work in space. They learn about other planets. The things they learn about life away from Earth may be very helpful in the future.

Judges are trained to understand the laws of our country. They must make many difficult decisions, such as how to punish people who break our laws.

Pilots spend many hours learning how to fly airplanes. They are ready to handle many types of emergencies.

Teachers spend years learning how to help others learn. There are teachers for every subject and for every age of student.

Directions: Draw a line between each job and the place you might find each person working.

doctor	space station
astronaut	school
judge	airport
pilot	hospital
teacher	court

Name: ______________________

Career Vocabulary

Directions: Read the sentence starters and complete each sentence.

1. A doctor goes to school for many years and learns all about the human body so that ______________________.
2. A ____________ helps children learn many different ____________, including reading, math, science and ______________________.
3. A ______________________ helps to put out fires, and must be very brave and ______________________.
4. Police officers wear ____________, carry ____________, and stop ______________________ from committing crimes.
5. A ______________________ makes lots of good things to eat, such as cookies, cakes and ____________, and might work in a ______________________.
6. A ______________________ milks cows, feeds chickens and grows crops such as ____________, ____________ and ____________.

What do you want to be when you grow up? ______________________

____

Why? ____

Name: ______________________

Ocean Animals Vocabulary

Directions: Use the word box to find the words hidden in the puzzle. The first one is done for you.

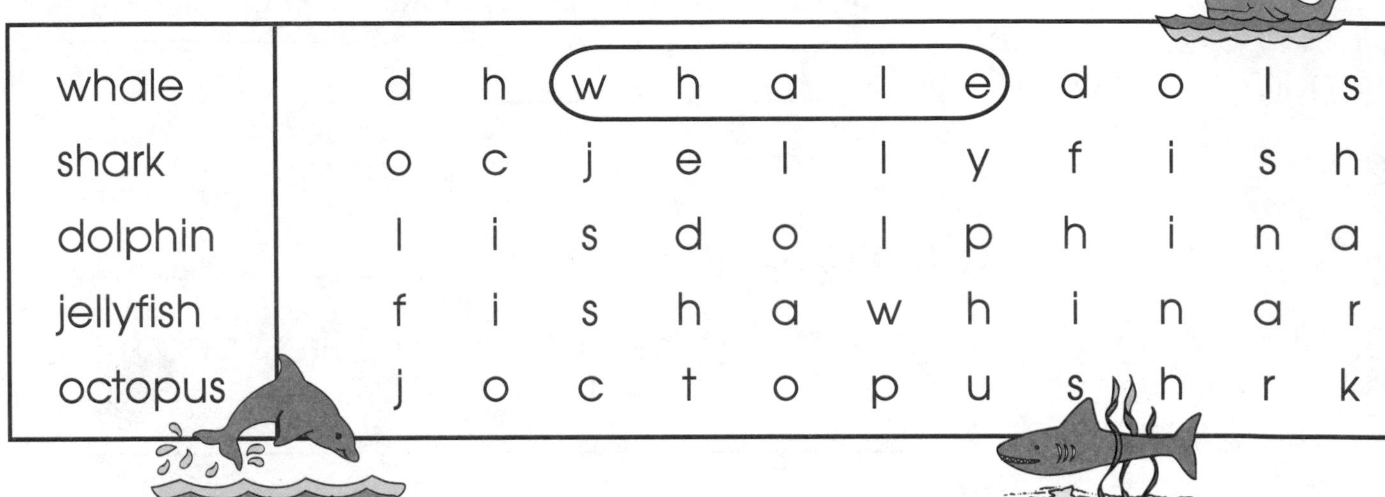

Word Box											
whale	d	h	w	h	a	l	e	d	o	l	s
shark	o	c	j	e	l	l	y	f	i	s	h
dolphin	l	i	s	d	o	l	p	h	i	n	a
jellyfish	f	i	s	h	a	w	h	i	n	a	r
octopus	j	o	c	t	o	p	u	s	h	r	k

Directions: Answer each riddle about ocean animals with a word from the word box.

1. I have a round, soft body with eight long arms. What am I? ______________________
2. I have many sharp teeth and tough gray skin. What am I? ______________________
3. I am the biggest animal in the ocean and the world. What am I? ______________________
4. My body looks like it is made of jelly. What am I? ______________________
5. People like me because I am friendly and can learn tricks. What am I? ______________________

Name: ______________________

Space Vocabulary

Directions: Unscramble each word. Use the numbers below the letters to tell you what order they belong in. Write the word by its definition.

i r t b o
4 2 5 3 1

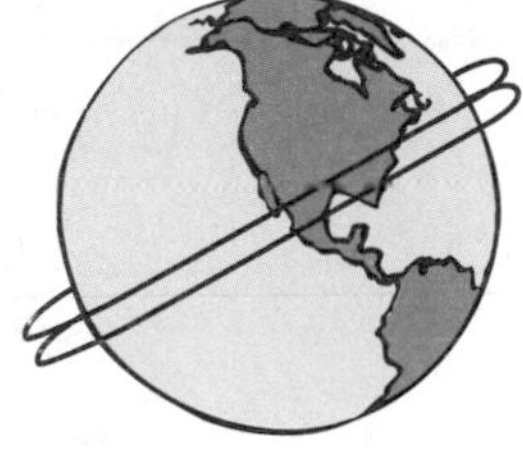

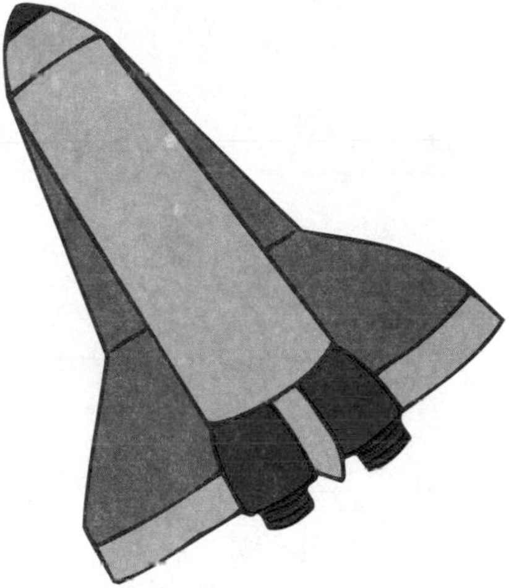

u t o n c w d n o
3 5 7 9 1 8 6 4 2

u l e f
2 4 3 1

a t s r a t n o u
7 9 2 4 1 3 6 5 8

t e h t s u l
5 7 2 4 1 3 6

A member of the team that flies a spaceship. ______________________

A rocket-powered spaceship that travels between Earth and space. ______________________

The material, such as gas, used for power. ______________________

The seconds just before take-off. ______________________

The path of a spaceship as it goes around Earth. ______________________

Name: ______________________

Weather Vocabulary

Directions: Use the weather words in the box to complete the sentences.

sunny	temperature	foggy	puddles	rainy
windy	rainbow	cloudy	lightning	snowy

1. My friends and I love ____________ days, because we can have snowball fights!
2. On __________ days, we like to stay indoors and play board games.
3. Today was hot and __________, so we went to the beach.
4. We didn't see the sun at all yesterday. It was __________ all day.
5. ____________ weather is perfect for flying kites.
6. It was so ____________, Mom had to use the headlights in the car so we wouldn't get lost.
7. While it was still raining, the sun began to shine and created a beautiful ______________ .
8. We like to jump in the ____________ after it rains.
9. ____________________ flashed across the sky during the thunderstorm.
10. The __________________ outside was so low, we needed to wear hats, mittens and scarves.

Name: 

Camping Vocabulary

Directions: Use the words below to find the hidden words in the puzzle. Look for the words horizontally, vertically, diagonally or backwards.

tent	fishing rod	bugs
sleeping bag	firewood	campground
flashlight	marshmallows	park
camper	lantern	nature
lake	swimming	canoe

s l e e p i n g b a g a c a r g
m a a b k f a j i n l c a p e n
a l a n t e r n t l x a n f a i
r e b d u n v a w s a r o i a m
s c m u j k r t e n t k e r o m
h p t x g w h u y l a u e e z i
m n e r l s i r e o g h v w r w
a z s u m t r e p m a c s o t s
l q r i k f o d o p c l p o l n
l e h y c a m p g r o u n d k e
o d o r g n i h s i f m f r u j
w f l a s h l i g h t d a t a y
s a f l a s h l i g n p n s i b

Name: ______________________

Vocabulary Word Lists

Directions: Complete the vocabulary word lists. Be creative!

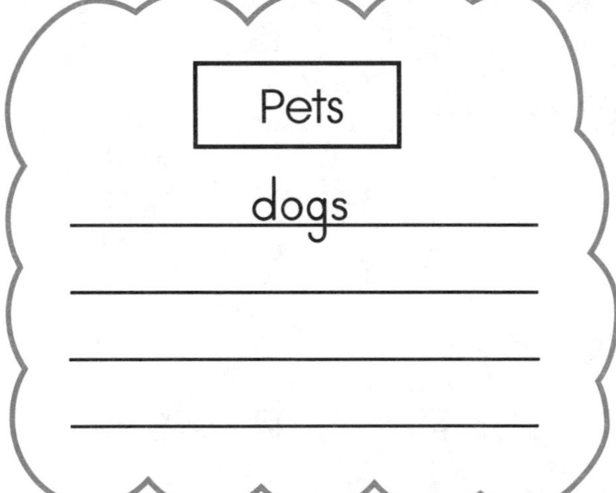

School Supplies

paper

____

____

____

What other things can you think of to list?

____

Name: ______________________

Reading Comprehension

Directions: Read the story. Then answer the questions.

George Washington Carver was an important American scientist. He was born in 1864, the son of a slave. When he was a baby, he was traded for a racehorse. After the slaves were freed, Carver worked to put himself through school.

Carver experimented with plants to find better ways to grow food. He learned that growing cotton for many years in the same field is bad for the soil. He taught farmers to grow peanuts and sweet potatoes for a few years to make the soil good again.

Carver also studied different ways to use peanuts and sweet potatoes. He found more than 300 ways to use peanuts!

1. Who was George Washington Carver? ______________________

____

2. What kinds of experiments did Carver try? ______________________

____

3. What crop did Carver find to be bad for the soil? ______________________

____

4. What crops did Carver find to be good for the soil? ______________________

____

Name: ____________________

Reading Comprehension

Directions: Read the story. Then answer the questions.

You can grow a **citrus** (SIT-russ) plant in your home. Citrus fruits include lemons, oranges and grapefruits. Collect seeds from a piece of fruit. Wash the seeds with water and let them dry for three days. Next, fill a four-inch pot with potting soil. You can buy soil at a garden store. Plant the seeds about one-inch deep and water thoroughly.

Plants need water and light to grow. Put your pot near a window where it can get light from the sun. Pour a little water on the soil after you plant the seeds. When the soil feels dry, water it again.

1. What are some kinds of citrus fruits? ____________________

____

2. How deep should you plant the seeds in the soil? ____________________

____

3. Name two things that plants need to grow.

1) ____________________ 2) ____________________

4. How do you know when to water your plant? ____________________

____

Name: ____________________

Reading Comprehension

Directions: Read the story. Then answer the questions.

Weed is the word used for any plant that grows where it is not wanted. Grasses that grow in your flower or vegetable garden are weeds. An unwanted flower growing in your lawn is also a weed. Dandelions are this kind of weed.

People do not plant weeds. They grow very fast. If you do not pull them out or kill them, weeds will crowd out the plants that you want to grow. The seeds of many kinds of weeds are spread by the wind. Birds and other animals also carry weed seeds.

1. A weed is any plant that grows ____________________

____.

2. One kind of flowering weed is the ____________________

____.

3. Two things that spread the seeds of weeds are

____________________ and ____________________.

Name: ______________________

Reading Comprehension

Directions: Read the story. Then answer the questions.

What is a **robot**? Does a robot do any of your work for you?

A robot is any machine that can do work without a person being needed to run it all the time. A dishwasher is a kind of robot. A clock radio is a robot, too. They may not look like the robots you see on television or read about in books, but they are.

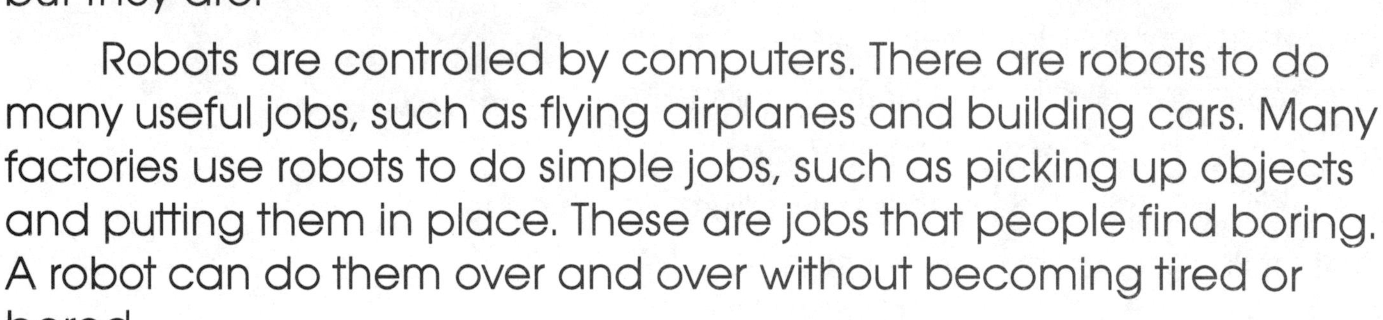

Robots are controlled by computers. There are robots to do many useful jobs, such as flying airplanes and building cars. Many factories use robots to do simple jobs, such as picking up objects and putting them in place. These are jobs that people find boring. A robot can do them over and over without becoming tired or bored.

1. What is a robot? ____

____.

2. Name two uses for robots.

1) ______________________ 2) ______________________

3. What controls a robot? ____

____.

Name: ______________________

Reading Comprehension

Directions: Read the story. Then answer the questions.

Almost anytime you look up at the sky, you can see clouds. **Clouds** are made up of little drops of water or ice. There are three main kinds of clouds.

Cirrus (SIR-es) clouds are thin and feathery. They are the highest clouds in the sky. They usually mean fair weather. But if they thicken, it could rain.

Cumulus (KUME-ya-les) clouds are puffy and cottony. Their shapes are always changing. You will see them low in the sky. They mean good weather. But piles of cumulus clouds make up **nimbus** clouds. These are black storm clouds. They are sometimes called thunderheads.

Stratus clouds are low in the sky, too. They look like wide, gray blankets. Drizzle and snow flurries fall from them.

1. What are clouds made of? ______________________

____

2. List three main kinds of clouds.

1) ______________________

2) ______________________

3) ______________________

Name: ____________________

Reading Comprehension

Directions: Look at the pictures of clouds. Complete each sentence with the name of the cloud described. Use page 35 to help you.

cirrus	nimbus	cumulus	stratus

1. I am a low, flat, gray cloud. I bring drizzles or snow flurries. I am a ____ cloud.

   ____

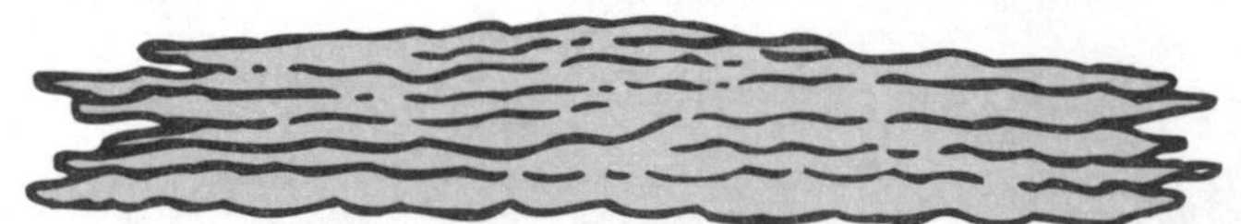

2. I am a black storm cloud. I am made up of many cumulus clouds. I have a flat top. I am a ____ cloud.

   ____

3. I am a thin, feathery cloud high in the sky. I usually mean good weather. I am a ____ cloud.

   ____

4. I am a puffy, cottony cloud. I won't ruin your picnic, because I mean fair weather. I am a ____ cloud.

   ____

Name: ____________________

Reading Comprehension

Directions: Read the story. Then answer the questions.

The giant panda lives in bamboo forests in the mountains of China. This is lucky, because bamboo is the panda's favorite food! Bamboo is a kind of woody grass. It grows to be very tall. Bamboo grows in tough shoots called stalks.

A panda may eat hundreds of stalks of bamboo in a day. One reason is that one stalk of bamboo isn't very filling! Another reason is that only the top on the stalk is tender enough to eat. Of course, pandas think bamboo is delicious!

1. Where do giant pandas live?

____

2. What is a panda's favorite food?

____

3. What is bamboo?

____

4. Write two reasons why pandas eat so many stalks of bamboo everyday.

   1) ____________________________________

   2) ____________________________________

Name: ___________________

Reading Comprehension

Directions: Read the story. Then answer the questions.

In 1972, the Chinese people gave two giant pandas to the American people. The pandas lived at the National Zoo in Washington, D.C. for many years. At the time, they were the only giant pandas living in America.

The girl panda's name was Ling-Ling. That means "cute little girl" in Chinese. She died in 1992. The boy panda's name is Hsing-Hsing (shing-shing). It means "new."

1. How many giant pandas lived in America?

____

2. Where did these pandas live?

____

3. What were the names of the giant pandas that came to America?

____

4. What do their names mean?

____

____

Name: ____________________

Reading Comprehension

Directions: Read the story. Then answer the questions.

Each year, as the hours of daylight grow shorter and colder weather comes, many types of trees lose their leaves. The falling of the leaves is so regular and amazing that the entire autumn season is called "fall."

The trees that lose their leaves are known as **deciduous** (dee-SID-you-us) trees. The word means "falling down." The leaves on these trees are wide, not like the needle-shaped leaves on pine and other **evergreen** trees. Trees lose water through their leaves, and wide leaves lose more water than the ones that look like needles. Water is very important to a tree. Because there is less water in the winter, the tree must drop its leaves to stay alive.

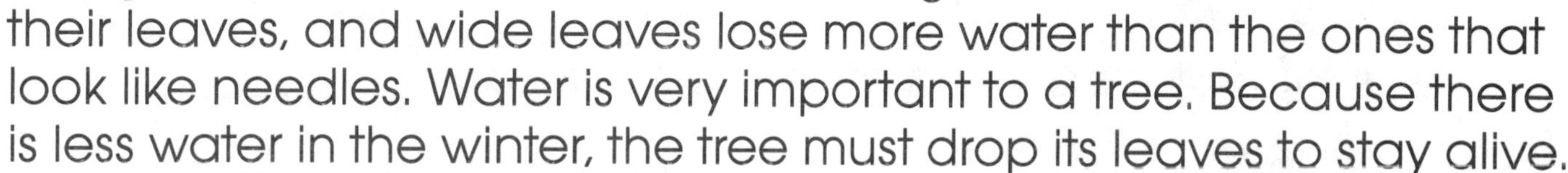

1. In what season do deciduous trees lose their leaves? ____________

2. What are the trees called that do not lose their leaves?

____

Circle the correct answer.

3. Deciduous trees have needle-shaped leaves. True False

4. Trees drop their leaves to save water. True False

Name: ____________________

Reading Comprehension

Directions: Read the story. Then answer the questions.

A tree has many living parts: roots, trunk, branches and leaves. The roots, trunk and branches grow each year. And every year new leaves grow on the branches. But there is a part of the tree that is not living. That part is the outer covering called the bark.

Bark is very hard and tough. It helps to protect the tree from harm. The bark stretches as the tree grows. On some trees, the bark stretches easily and looks smooth. On other trees, it doesn't stretch very easily. As these trees grow, the bark cracks and looks rough and bumpy.

1. What is the outer covering of the tree called? ____________________

Circle the correct answer.

2. If the bark of the tree stretches easily, the bark looks bumpy. True False

3. The bark helps to protect the tree from harm. Can you think of ways that a tree could be harmed?

____

____

____

Name: ____________________

Reading Comprehension

Directions: Read the story. Then answer the questions.

Have you ever seen a tree that has been cut down? If so, you may have seen many circles in the trunk. These are called the **annual rings**. You can tell how old a tree is by counting these rings.

Trees have these rings because they grow a new layer of wood every year. The new layer grows right below the bark. In a year when there is a lot of rain and sunlight, the tree grows faster; the annual ring that year will be thick. When there is not much rain or sunlight, the tree grows slower and the ring is thin.

Circle the correct answer.

1. The annual ring of a tree tells how big the tree is.

   True False

2. Each year, a new layer of wood grows on top of the bark.

   True False

3. In a year with lots of rain and sunlight, the annual ring will be thick.

   True False

4. Trees grow faster when there is more rain and sunlight.

   True False

5. How old was the tree on this page? ____________________

Name: ____________________

Review

Directions: Use a word from the word box to finish each sentence and fill in the puzzle.

bark	branches	leaves	living	rings	roots	trunk

Across:

1. The bark of the tree is not alive, but the branches, roots and trunk are all ________ .
2. The parts of the tree that grow out of the trunk are the ________ .
3. The parts of the tree that grow underground are the ________ .
5. You can tell how old a tree is by counting the annual ________ .

Down:

1. The ________ often change color and fall off of the tree in autumn.
2. The outer covering that protects the tree is called the ________ .
4. The big center part of the tree is the ________ .

Name: ______________________

Sequencing

Directions: Look at the mixed-up pictures. Read all of the sentences. Then write 1, 2, 3 or 4 by each sentence to tell the order of the story.

________ Dave washed the car with rags.

________ He put soap and water in a bucket.

________ Dave drove his car through a big mud puddle.

________ He rinsed the soap off of the car with a hose.

Name: ____________________

Sequencing

Directions: Fill in the blank spaces with what comes next in the series. The first one is done for you.

year	Wednesday	day	sixth	large
twenty	February	night	seventeen	mile
paragraph	winter	ocean		

1. Sunday, Monday, Tuesday, ____Wednesday____
2. third, fourth, fifth, ____________________
3. November, December, January, ____________________
4. tiny, small, medium, ____________________
5. fourteen, fifteen, sixteen, ____________________
6. morning, afternoon, evening, ____________________
7. inch, foot, yard, ____________________
8. day, week, month, ____________________
9. spring, summer, autumn, ____________________
10. five, ten, fifteen, ____________________
11. letter, word, sentence, ____________________
12. second, minute, hour, ____________________
13. stream, lake, river, ____________________

Name: ______________________________

Sequencing

Directions: Read each story. Circle the phrase that tells what happened before.

1. Beth is very happy now that she has someone to play with. She hopes that her new sister will grow up quickly!

   A few days ago . . .

   Beth was sick.

   Beth's mother had a baby.

   Beth got a new puppy.

2. Sara tried to mend the tear. She used a needle and thread to sew up the hole.

   While playing, Sara had . . .

   broken her bicycle.

   lost her watch.

   torn her shirt.

3. The movers took John's bike off the truck and put it in the garage. Next, they moved his bed into his new bedroom.

   John's family . . .

   bought a new house.

   went on vacation.

   bought a new truck.

4. Katie picked out a book about dinosaurs. Jim, who likes sports, chose two books about baseball.

   Katie and Jim . . .

   went to the library.

   went to the playground.

   went to the grocery.

Name: ______________________

Sequencing

Directions: Read each story. Circle the sentence that tells what might happen next.

1. Sam and Judy picked up their books and left the house. They walked to the bus stop. They got on a big yellow bus.

   What will Sam and Judy do next?

   They will go to school.

   They will visit their grandmother.

   They will go to the store.

2. Maggie and Matt were playing in the snow. They made a snow–man with a black hat and a red scarf. Then the sun came out.

   What might happen next?

   It will snow again.

   They will play in the sandbox.

   The snowman will melt.

3. Megan put on a big floppy hat and funny clothes. She put green make-up on her face.

   What will Megan do next?

   She will go to school.

   She will go to a costume party.

   She will go to bed.

4. Mike was eating a hot dog. Suddenly he smelled smoke. He turned and saw a fire on the stove.

   What will Mike do next?

   He will watch the fire.

   He will call for help.

   He will finish his hot dog.

Name: ____________________

Sequencing

Directions: Number these sentences from 1 to 6 to show the correct order of the story.

It is almost Valentine's Day . . .

_____ She cut the paper into heart shapes and decorated them.

_____ She put names and addresses on the envelopes.

__1__ Sally wanted to make valentines for her friends.

_____ She got out paper, glue and scissors.

_____ She put the valentines in the mailbox.

_____ She bought envelopes to put them in.

The astronauts are going to the moon!

_____ The spaceship takes the astronauts to the moon.

__1__ The astronauts must get into their space suits.

_____ Then the countdown to take-off starts.

_____ They climb into the spaceship.

_____ Rockets blast the spaceship into space.

_____ The astronauts walk on the moon.

Name: ____________________

Sequencing

Directions: Number these sentences from 1 to 5 to show the correct order of the story.

Building a Treehouse

_____ They had a beautiful treehouse!

_____ They got wood and nails.

__1__ Jay and Lisa planned to build a treehouse.

_____ Now, they like to eat lunch in their treehouse.

_____ Lisa and Jay worked in the backyard for three days building the treehouse.

A School Play

_____ Everyone clapped when the curtain closed.

_____ The girl who played Snow White came onto the stage.

_____ All the other school children went to the gym to see the play.

_____ The stage curtain opened.

__1__ The third grade was going to put on a play about Snow White.

Name: ____________________

Sequencing

Directions: Number these sentences from 1 to 8 to show the correct order of the story.

_____ Jack's father called the family doctor.

_____ Jack felt much better as his parents drove him home.

_____ Jack woke up in the middle of the night with a terrible pain in his stomach.

_____ The doctor told Jack's father to take Jack to the hospital.

_____ Jack called his parents to come help him.

_____ At the hospital, the doctors examined Jack. They said the problem was not serious. They told Jack's parents that he could go home.

_____ Jack's mother took his temperature. He had a fever of 103 degrees.

_____ On the way to the hospital, Jack rested in the backseat. He was worried.

Name: ____________________

Review

Directions: Read the story. Then follow the directions.

The Magnifying Glass

Timmy's grandfather was reading the newspaper. He held something in his hand as he read. "What's that, Grandpa?" asked Timmy. "It's a magnifying glass to help me see the words better," said Grandpa. He showed Timmy how holding the glass over a word made the word look bigger.

Timmy looked at a fly under the magnifying glass. The fly looked big! Timmy could even see the eye of the fly. "It's like magic!" he said.

Timmy wanted to explore the yard with Grandpa's magic glass. "Let's go to the store and buy one for you," said Grandpa. "Then I can finish reading my newspaper!"

Directions: Number these sentences from 1 to 5 to show the correct order of the story.

________ Timmy looked at a fly under the magnifying glass.

________ Timmy's grandfather was reading.

________ Grandpa showed Timmy how the magnifying glass worked.

________ Timmy wanted to take the magnifying glass outside.

________ Grandpa is going to buy Timmy a magnifying glass.

Name: ____________________

Noting Details

Directions: Read the story. Then answer the questions.

Thomas Edison was one of America's greatest inventors. An **inventor** thinks up new machines and new ways of doing things. Edison was born in Milan, Ohio in 1847. He went to school for only three months. His teacher thought he was not very smart because he asked so many questions.

Edison liked to experiment. He had many wonderful ideas. He invented the light bulb and the phonograph (record player).

Thomas Edison died in 1931, but we still use many of his inventions today.

1. What is an inventor?

____

2. Where was Thomas Edison born?

____

3. How long did he go to school?

____

4. What are two of Edison's inventions?

____

Name: ____________________

Noting Details

Directions: Read the story. Then answer the questions.

The giant panda is much smaller than a brown bear or a polar bear. In fact, a horse weighs about four times as much as a giant panda. So why is it called "giant"? It is giant next to another kind of panda called the red panda.

The red panda also lives in China. The red panda is about the size of a fox. It has a long, fluffy, striped tail and beautiful reddish fur. It looks very much like a raccoon.

Many people think the giant pandas are bears. They look like bears. Even the word panda is Chinese for "white bear." But because of its relationship to the red panda, many scientists now believe that the panda is really more like a raccoon!

1. Why is the giant panda called "giant"?

____

2. Where does the red panda live?

____

3. How big is the red panda?

____

4. What animal does the red panda look like?

____

5. What does the word panda mean?

____

Name: ____________________

Noting Details

Directions: Read the story. Then answer the questions.

Giant pandas do not live in families like people do. The only pandas that live together are mothers and their babies. Newborn pandas are very tiny and helpless. They weigh only five ounces when they are born—about the weight of a stick of butter! They are born with their eyes closed, and they have no teeth.

It takes about three years for a panda to grow up. When full grown, a giant panda weighs about 300 pounds and is five to six feet tall. Once a panda is grown up, it leaves its mother and goes off to live by itself.

1. What pandas live together? ____________________

____

2. How much do pandas weigh when they are born? ____________________

____

3. Why do newborn pandas live with their mothers? ____________________

____

4. When is a panda full grown? ____________________

____

5. How big is a grown-up panda? ____________________

Name: 

Following Directions

Directions: Learning to follow directions is very important. Use the map to find your way to different houses.

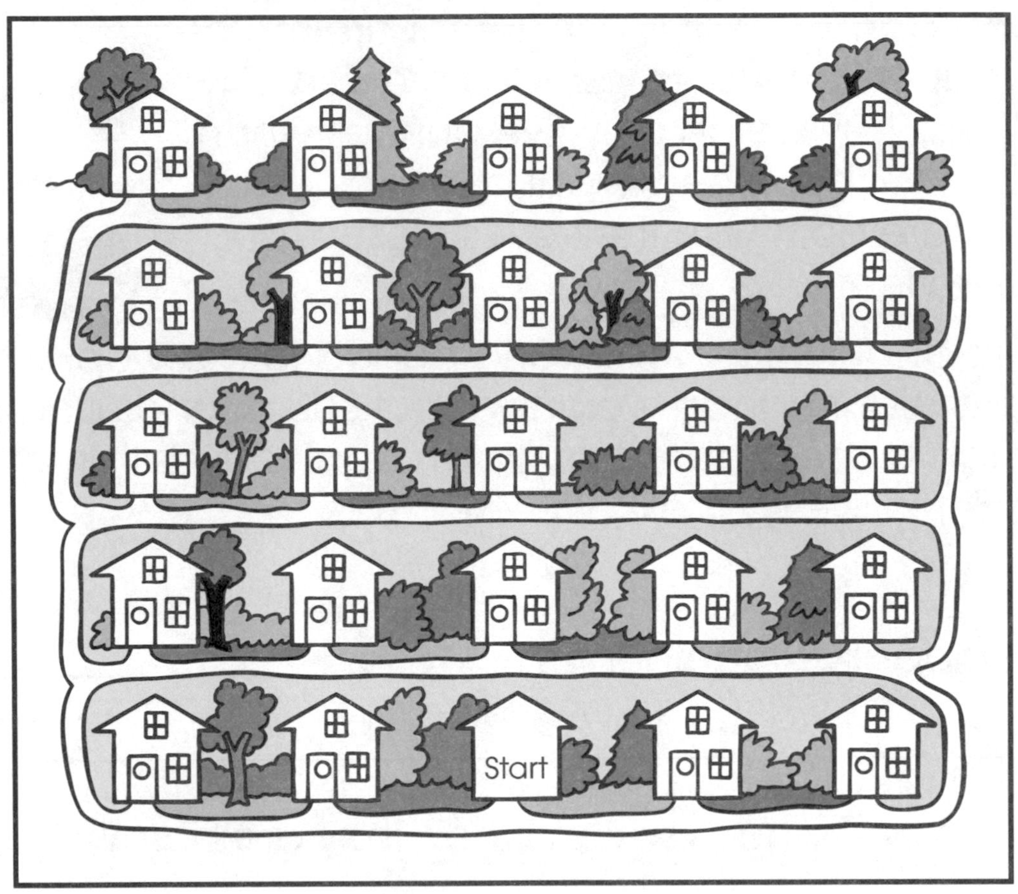

1. Color the start house yellow.
2. Go north 2 houses, and east two houses.
3. Go north 2 houses, and west 4 houses.
4. Color the house green.

5. Start at the yellow house.
6. Go east 1 house, and north 3 houses.
7. Go west 3 houses, and south 3 houses.
8. Color the house blue.

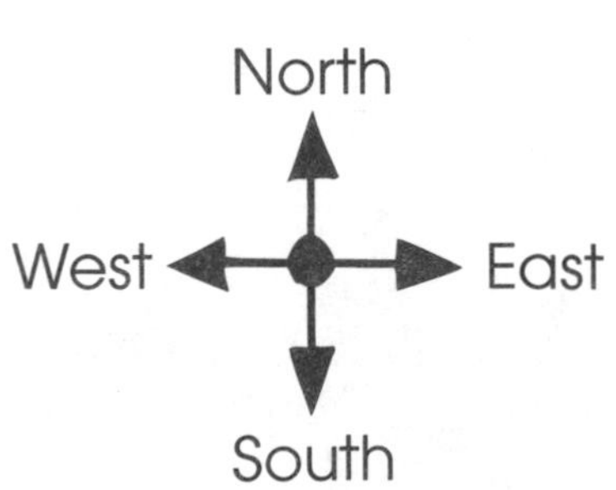

Name: ______________________

Following Directions

Origami is the Japanese art of paper folding. No scissors or glue are needed.

Directions: Use a piece of plain paper. Follow the steps listed below.

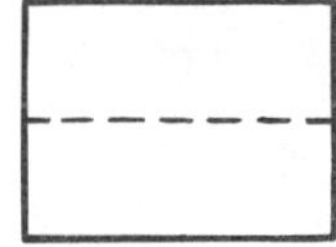

1. Fold the paper in half the long way, crease and unfold.

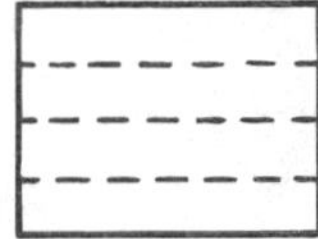

2. Fold the sides up to the middle crease. Keep folded.

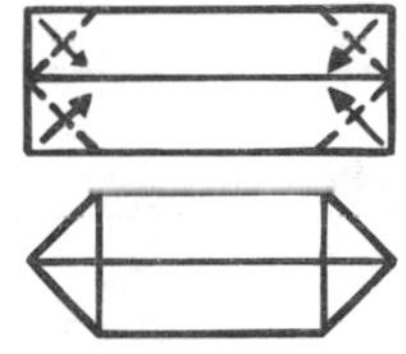

3. Fold the corners down to the middle.

4. Fold the corners down to the middle again.

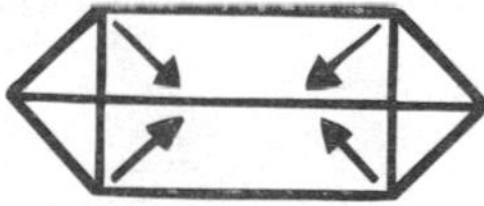

5. Fold the points down to the middle.

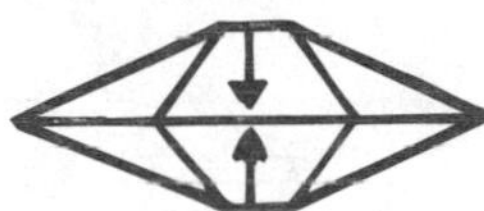

6. Open the middle and turn it inside out for a boat, or flip it over and wear it as a hat!

What else can you make using origami?

Name: ______________________

Following Directions

Directions: How many words can you find in the letters below? Go from left to right. Write the words in the blank spaces. The first two are done for you.

s o a p e t o e a t w i g l o w e t a n o t h e r e d i p a n d a m p

1. so
2. soap
3. ______
4. ______
5. ______
6. ______
7. ______
8. ______
9. ______
10. ______
11. ______
12. ______
13. ______
14. ______
15. ______
16. ______
17. ______
18. ______
19. ______
20. ______
21. ______
22. ______
23. ______
24. ______

Super Word Finder!

25. ______
26. ______
27. ______
28. ______

You're the best!

29. ______
30. ______
31. ______
32. ______

Name: ____________________

Following Directions

Directions: Read each sentence and do what it says to do.

1. Count the syllables in each word. Write the number on the line by the word.
2. Draw a line between the two words in each compound word.
3. Draw a circle around each name of a month.
4. Draw a box around each food word.
5. Draw an **X** on each noise word.
6. Draw a line under each day of the week.
7. Write the three words from the list you did not use. Draw a picture of each of those words.

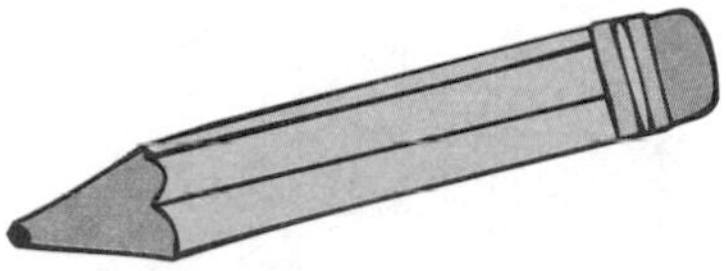

______ April	______ vegetable	______ tablecloth
______ bang	______ June	______ meat
______ sidewalk	______ Saturday	______ crash
______ astronaut	______ March	______ jingle
______ moon	______ cardboard	______ rocket
______ Friday	______ fruit	______ Monday

____________________ ____________________ ____________________

MASTER SKILLS READING

Name: ____________________

Following Directions

Directions: Look at the calendar page. Read each sentence and do what it says to do.

___ ___ b r ___ ___ r y						
Sunday	**Mon___**	**Tuesday**	**______**	**Th___day**	**Friday**	**Saturday**
1	2	3			6	
8	9	10	11	12		14
15				19	20	21
	23					28

1. Guess the month. It is a winter month, and it is the month with the fewest days. Write the missing letters in the name on the top line.
2. Write the missing numbers for the dates.
3. Write the name of the missing day where it belongs.
4. Write the missing letters in the names of two days.
5. Circle the dates that will be Saturdays.
6. The 2nd is Groundhog Day. Draw a brown **X** in that square.
7. The 12th is Abraham Lincoln's birthday. Draw a black top hat in that square.
8. The 14th is Valentine's Day. Draw a red heart in that square.
9. George Washington's birthday is on the 22nd. Draw a red cherry in that square.

Name: ____________________

Following Directions

Following directions carefully and doing things in the correct order are very important when you are following a recipe.

Directions: Follow the recipe to make goop. Then answer the questions.

Goop

1. Mix equal parts of cornstarch and water. Begin with 1 cup each.
2. Mix it the best you can. Watch out — it's tricky!
3. Pour the mixture onto a tray.
4. Try to squeeze it, pick it up and draw on it.
5. Have fun!

1. What does the goop look like? ____________________

2. How does the goop feel? ____________________

3. What does the goop smell like? ____________________

4. Does your goop make any noise? ____________________

Name: ______________________

Review

Directions: Read the sentences. Follow the directions to fill in the boxes and discover the secret message.

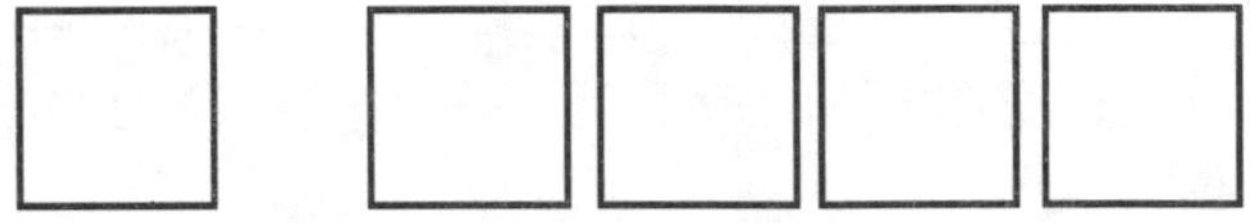

1. In the first row of boxes put:
    - the last letter in the word **model** in the second box.
    - the first vowel in the word **message** in the fifth box.
    - the second vowel in the word **cutting** in the first and third boxes.
    - the last consonant in the word **pick** in the fourth box.

2. In the second row of boxes put:
    - the vowel that appears twice in the word **pleasant** in the fifth box.
    - the second consonant in the word **breath** in the third box.
    - the silent letter in the word **blade** in the fourth box.
    - the double consonant in the word **middle** in the sixth box.
    - the vowel that you hear in the word **boat** in the second box.
    - the consonant at the end of the word **giant** in the first box.

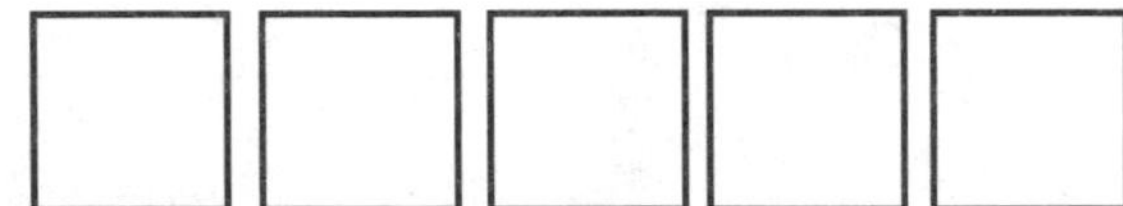

3. In the third row of boxes put:
    - the third consonant in the word **cheese** in the fifth box.
    - the fourth vowel in the word **delicious** in the second and third box.
    - the silent letter in the word **crumb** in the first box.
    - the silent consonant in the word **knife** in the fourth box.

Name: ____________________

Main Idea

The main idea of a story is what the story is mostly about.

Directions: Read the story. Then answer the questions.

A tree is more than the enormous plant you see growing in your yard. A large part of the tree grows under the ground. This part is called the roots. If the tree is very big and very old, the roots may stretch down 100 feet!

The roots hold the tree in the ground. The roots do another important job for the tree. They gather minerals and water from the soil to feed the tree so it will grow. Most land plants, including trees, could not live without roots to support and feed them.

1. The main idea of this story is:

   The roots of a tree are underground.

   The roots do important jobs for the tree.

2. Where are the roots of a tree? ____________________

Circle the correct answer.

3. The roots help to hold the tree up. True False

4. Name two things the roots collect from the soil for the tree.

   1) ____________________ 2) ____________________

Name: ____________________

Main Idea

Directions: Read about spiders. Then answer the questions.

Many people think spiders are insects, but they are not. Spiders are the same size as insects, and they look like insects in some ways. But there are three ways to tell a spider from an insect. Insects have six legs, and spiders have eight legs. Insects have antennae, but spiders do not. An insect's body is divided into three parts; a spider's body is divided into only two parts.

1. The main idea of this story is:

   Spiders are like insects.

   Spiders are like insects in some ways, but they are not insects.

2. What are three ways to tell a spider from an insect?

   1) ______________________________

   2) ______________________________

   3) ______________________________

Circle the correct answer.

3. Spiders are the same size as insects. True False

Name: ______________________

Main Idea

Directions: Read about the giant panda. Then answer the questions.

Giant pandas are among the world's favorite animals. They look like big, cuddly stuffed toys. There are not very many pandas left in the world. You may have to travel a long way to see one.

The only place on Earth where pandas live in the wild is in the bamboo forests of the mountains of China. It is hard to see pandas in the forest because they are very shy. They hide among the many bamboo trees. It also is hard to see pandas because there are so few of them. Scientists think there may be less than 1,000 pandas living in the mountains of China.

1. Write a sentence that tells the main idea of this story:

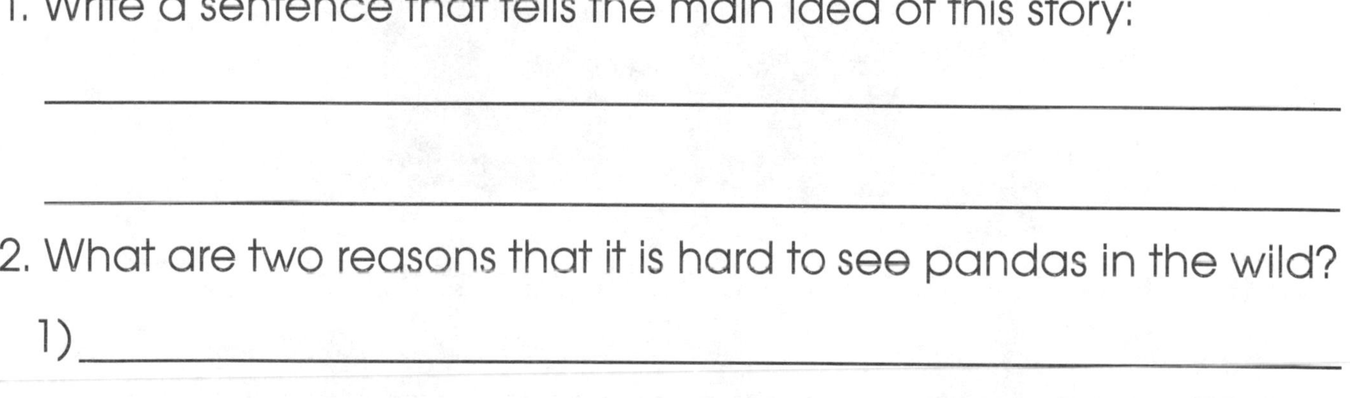

____

____

2. What are two reasons that it is hard to see pandas in the wild?

   1) ____

   2) ____

3. How many pandas are believed to be living in the mountains of China?

____

Master Skills Reading

Name: ____________________

Main Idea

Directions: Read the story. Then answer the questions.

Because bamboo is very important to pandas, they have special body features that help them eat it. The panda's front foot is like a hand. But, instead of four fingers and a thumb, the panda has five fingers and an extra-long wrist bone. With its special front foot, the panda can easily pick up the stalks of bamboo. It also can hold the bamboo more tightly than it could with a hand like ours.

Bamboo stalks are very tough. The panda uses its big heavy head, large jaws and big back teeth to chew. Pandas eat the bamboo first by peeling the outside of the stalk. They do this by moving their front feet from side to side while holding the stalk in their teeth. Then they bite off a piece of the bamboo and chew it with their strong jaws.

1. Write a sentence that tells the main idea of this story.

____

2. Instead of four fingers and a thumb, the panda has

____

3. Bamboo is very tender. True False

Name: ______________________

Review

Directions: Read the story. Then answer the questions.

Hsing-Hsing lives in a special Panda House in the National Zoo. He has a large air-conditioned cage (the temperature is kept at 50 degrees Fahrenheit) and a sleeping den. Hsing-Hsing can play in a big yard. The yard has bamboo trees growing in it.

It is very expensive to feed pandas. Besides bamboo, they also like rice, apples, bone meal, honey, carrots, cat food and dog biscuits, sweet potatoes, cantaloupes and grass. It costs about as much to feed two pandas as it does to feed three elephants!

1. Write a sentence that tells the main idea of this story.

____

____

2. At what temperature do you need to keep panda cages?

____

3. Name three things other than bamboo that pandas like to eat.

1) ____________________ 3) ____________________

2) ____________________

4. How expensive is it to feed two pandas?

____

Name: ____________________

Review

Directions: Read the story. Then answer the questions.

There are many different kinds of robots. One special kind of robot takes the place of people in guiding airplanes and ships. They are called "automatic pilots." These robots are really computers programmed to do just one special job. They have the information to control the speed and direction of the plane or ship.

Robots are used for many jobs in which a person can't get too close because of danger, such as in exploding a bomb. Robots can be controlled from a distance. This is called "remote control." These robots are very important in studying space. In the future, robots will be used to work on space stations and on other planets.

1. The main idea of this story is:

____

____

2. Why are robots good in dangerous jobs?

____

3. What is "remote control"?

____

4. What will robots be used for in the future?

____

What would you have a robot do for you?

____

Name: ______________________

Inference

Inference is using logic to figure out what is not directly told.

Directions: Read the story. Then answer the questions.

Many thousands of people go to the National Zoo each year to see Hsing-Hsing. Sometimes, there are as many as 1,000 visitors in one hour! Like all pandas, Hsing-Hsing spends most of his time sleeping. But because pandas are so rare, most people think it is exciting to see even a sleeping panda!

1. Popular means well-liked. Do you think giant pandas are popular?

____

2. What clue do you have that pandas are popular?

____

3. What do most visitors see Hsing-Hsing doing?

____

Name: ______________________

Inference

Directions: Read the messages on the memo board. Then answer the questions.

1. What kind of lesson does Katie have? ______________________
2. What time is Amy's birthday party? ______________________
3. What kind of appointment does Jeff have on September 3rd? ______________________
4. Who goes to choir practice? ______________________
5. Where is Dad's meeting? ______________________
6. What time does Jeff go to the doctor? ______________________

Name: ____________________

Drawing Conclusions

Directions: On the top line by each picture, write the word from the word box that describes the person in the picture. Then write a clue from the picture that helped you decide.

chef	astronaut	teacher

Answer: ____________________

Clue: ____________________

Answer: ____________________

Clue: ____________________

Answer: ____________________

Clue: ____________________

Name: ____________________

Reading for Information

Directions: Read the story. List the four steps or changes a caterpillar goes through as it becomes a butterfly. Draw the stages in the boxes at the bottom of the page.

The Life Cycle of the Butterfly

One of the most magical changes in nature is the metamorphosis of a caterpillar. There are four stages in the transformation. The first stage is the embryonic stage. This is the stage in which tiny eggs are deposited on a leaf. The second stage is the larvae stage. We usually think of caterpillars at this stage. Many people like to capture the caterpillars hoping that while they have the caterpillar, it will turn into pupa. Another name for the pupa stage is the cocoon stage. Many changes happen inside the cocoon that we cannot see. Inside the cocoon, the caterpillar is changing into an adult. The adult breaks out of the cocoon as a beautiful butterfly!

1. ____________________

2. ____________________

3. ____________________

4. ____________________

Life Cycle of the Butterfly

Name: ____________________

Reading for Information: The Food Pyramid

Eating foods that are good for you is very important for you to stay healthy.

Directions: List different foods or draw pictures to go in each group.

Food Pyramid (per day)

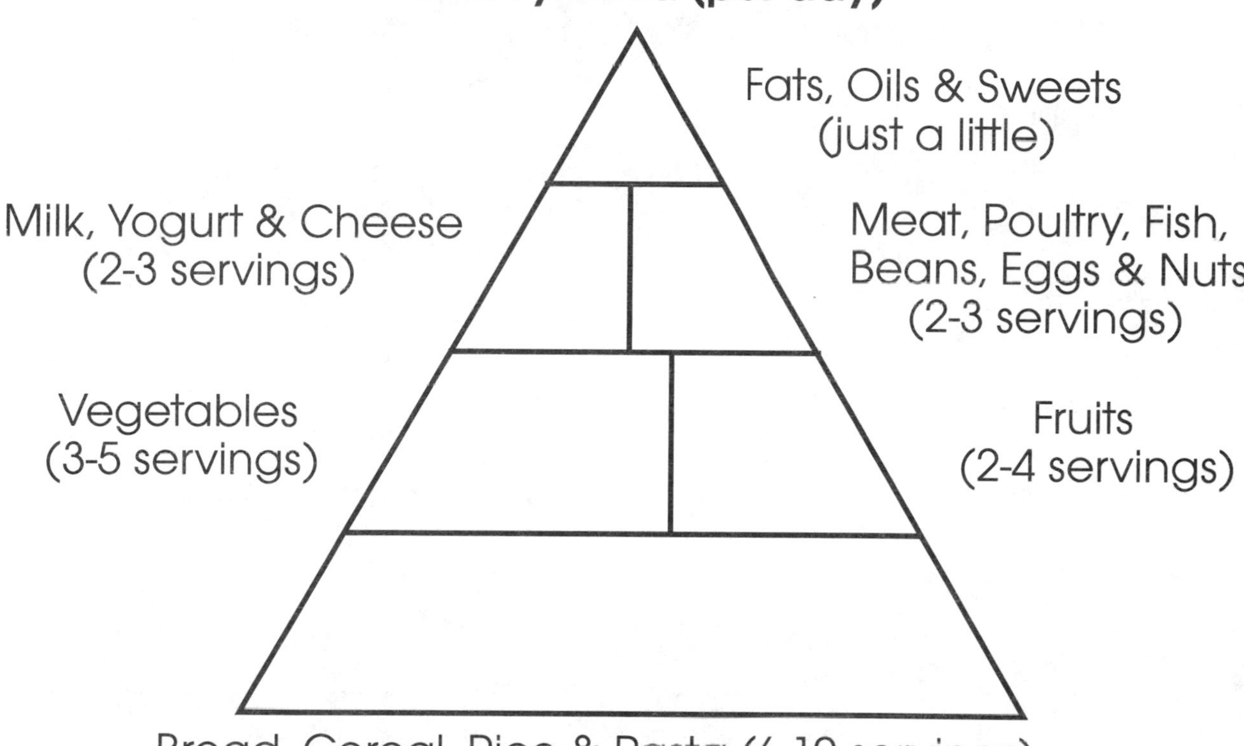

Circle the correct answers.

1. You should eat as many sweets as possible. True False
2. You should eat 6-10 servings of the bread group per day. True False
3. 3-5 servings of meat is recommended per day. True False
4. What is your favorite food? ____________________

Name: ______________________

Reading for Information

Telephone books contain information about people's addresses and phone numbers. They also list business addresses and phone numbers. The information in a telephone book is listed in alphabetical order.

Directions: Use your telephone book to find the following places in your area. Ask your mom or dad for help if you need it.

Can you find . . .

	Name	Phone number
. . . a pizza place?	______________	______________
. . . a bicycle store?	______________	______________
. . . a pet shop?	______________	______________
. . . a toy store?	______________	______________
. . . a water park?	______________	______________

What other telephone numbers would you like to have?

____

Name: ______________________

Reading for Information: Dictionaries

Dictionaries contain meanings and pronunciations of words. The words in a dictionary are listed in alphabetical order. Guide words appear at the top of each dictionary page. They help us know at a glance what words are on each page.

Directions: Place the words in alphabetical order.

apple	dog	crab	ear
book	atlas	cake	frog
egg	drip	coat	crib

Name: ____________________

Reading for Information: Newspapers

A newspaper has many parts. Some of the parts of a newspaper are:

- banner — the name of the paper
- lead story — the top news item
- caption — sentences under the picture which give information about the picture
- sports — scores and information on current sports events
- comics — drawings that tell funny stories
- editorial — an article by the editor expressing an opinion about something
- ads — paid advertisements
- weather — information about the weather
- advice column — letters from readers asking for help with a problem
- movie guides — a list of movies and movie times
- obituary — information about people who have died

Directions: Match the newspaper sections below with their definitions.

banner	an article by the editor
lead story	sentences under pictures
caption	movies and movie times
editorial	the name of the paper
movies	information about people who have died
obituary	the top news item

Name: ____________________

Newspaper Writing

Directions: Use the front page below to create a newspaper story about Cinderella.

♥ ______________________________ ♥

(banner)

Glass Slipper Found!

(lead story)

____

____

____

____

____

Evil Stepmothers: What do you think?

(editorial)

____

____

____

____

Today's Weather:

____

____

____

Draw a picture

(caption) ______________________________

____

Classified Ads: Wanted!

____

____

____

Advice:

Dear Fairy Godmother,

I want to go to the ball, and my stepmother won't let me go. What should I do?

____

____

____

Name: ____________________

Newspaper Writing

A good news story gives us important information. It answers the questions:

WHO? WHY? WHAT?

WHERE? HOW? WHEN?

Directions: Think about the story "Little Red Riding Hood." Answer the following questions about the story.

Who are the characters? ____________________

____

What is the story about? ____________________

____

Why does Red go to Granny's house? ____________________

____

Where does the story take place? ____________________

____

When did she go to Granny's house? ____________________

____

How did the Wolf greet Red? ____________________

____

Name: ____________________

Fantasy and Reality

Something that is **real** could actually happen. Something that is **fantasy** is not real. It could not happen.

Examples: Real: Dogs can bark.
Fantasy: Dogs can fly.

Directions: Look at the sentences below. Write **real** or **fantasy** next to each sentence.

1. My cat can talk to me. ____________
2. Witches ride brooms and cast spells. ____________
3. Dad can mow the lawn. ____________
4. I ride a magic carpet to school. ____________
5. I have a man-eating tree. ____________
6. My sandbox has toys in it. ____________
7. Mom can bake chocolate chip cookies. ____________
8. Mark's garden has tomatoes and corn in it. ____________
9. Jack grows candy and ice cream in his garden. ____________
10. I make my bed everyday. ____________

Write your own **real** sentence. ____________________

____

Write your own **fantasy** sentence. ____________________

____

Name: ______________________

Compound Words

A compound word is two small words put together to make one new word. Compound words are usually divided into syllables between the two words.

Directions: Read the words. Then divide them into syllables. The first one is done for you.

1. playground play ground
2. sailboat ______________
3. doghouse ______________
4. dishpan ______________
5. pigpen ______________
6. outdoors ______________
7. beehive ______________
8. airplane ______________
9. cardboard ______________
10. nickname ______________
11. hilltop ______________
12. broomstick ______________
13. sunburn ______________
14. oatmeal ______________
15. campfire ______________
16. somewhere ______________
17. starfish ______________
18. birthday ______________
19. sidewalk ______________
20. seashore ______________

Name: ____________________

Compound Words

Directions: Read the compound words in the word box. Then use them to answer the questions. The first one is done for you.

sailboat	blueberry	bookcase	tablecloth	beehive
dishpan	pigpen	classroom	playground	bedtime
broomstick	treetop	fireplace	newspaper	sunburn

Which compound word means . . .

1. a case for books? bookcase
2. a berry that is blue? ____________
3. a hive for bees? ____________
4. a place for fires? ____________
5. a pen for pigs? ____________
6. a room for a class? ____________
7. a pan for dishes? ____________
8. a boat to sail? ____________
9. a paper for news? ____________
10. a burn from the sun? ____________
11. the top of a tree? ____________
12. a stick for a broom? ____________
13. the time to go to bed? ____________
14. a cloth for the table? ____________
15. ground to play on? ____________

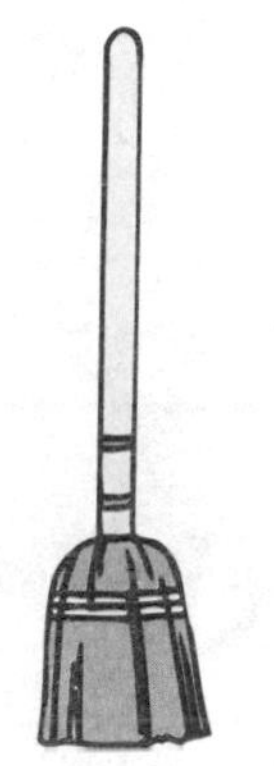

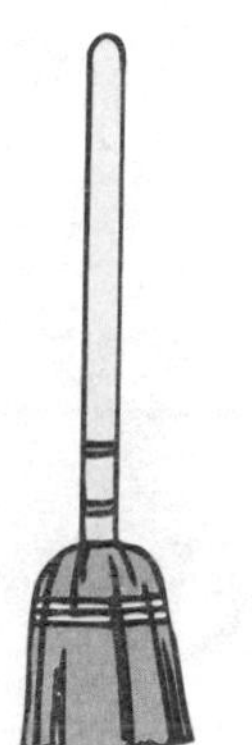

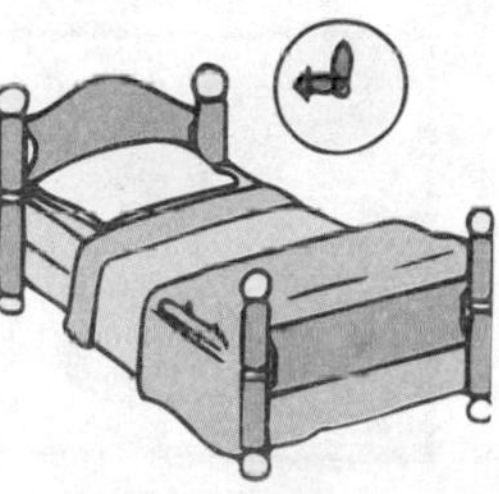

Name: ______________________

Homophones

Homophones are words that sound alike but have different meanings. The spellings are usually different, too.

Example: write and **right** are homophones.

Directions: Look at the pictures. Circle the word that tells what it is. The first one is done for you.

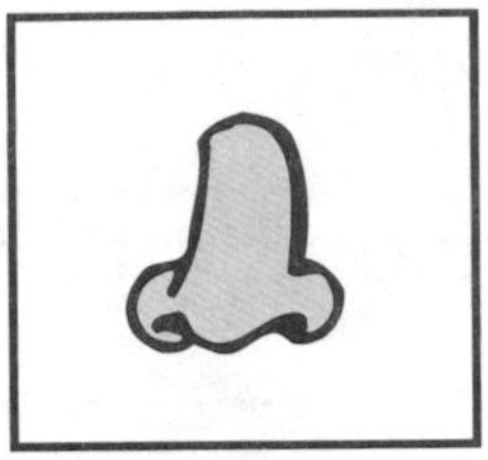

(nose) knows	ate eight	sew so
flower flour	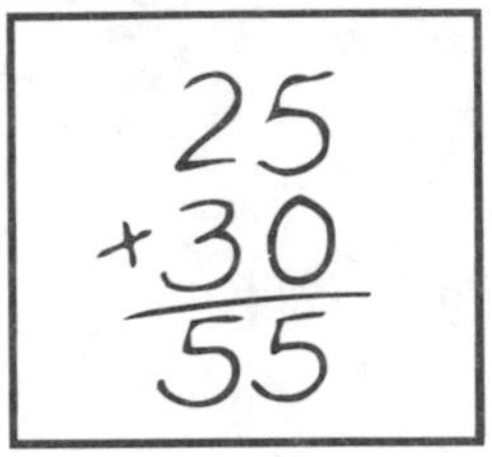 25 + 30 = 55 sum some	hare hair
four for	I eye	toe tow
deer dear	bear bare	cents sense

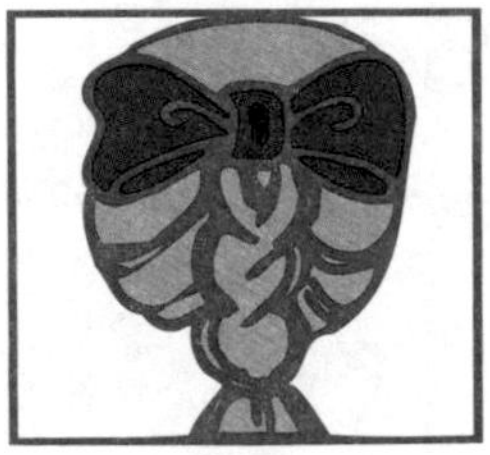

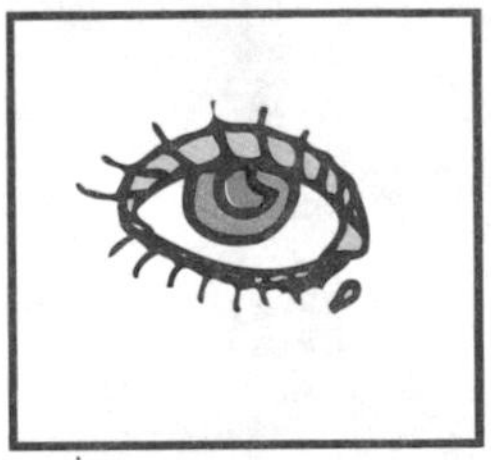

Name: ____________________

Homophones

Directions: Circle the correct word to complete each sentence. Then write the word on the line.

1. I am going to __________ a letter to my grandmother.
   right, write
2. Draw a circle around the __________ answer.
   right, write
3. Wait an ________ before going swimming.
   our, hour
4. This is ________ house.
   our, hour
5. He got a __________ from his garden.
   beat, beet
6. Our football team __________ that team.
   beat, beet
7. Go to the store and ________ a loaf of bread.
   by, buy
8. We will drive ________ your house.
   by, buy
9. It will be trouble if the dog __________ the cat.
   seas, sees
10. They sailed the seven __________ .
    seas, sees
11. We have ___________ cars in the garage.
    to, too, two
12. I am going ___________ the zoo today.
    to, too, two
13. My little brother is going, __________.
    to, too, two

Name: ______________________

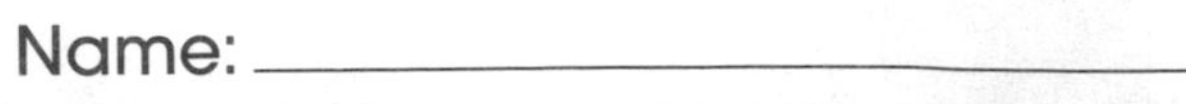

Review

Directions: Solve the puzzle.

doctor
shark
by
dolphin
orbit
beehive
earthquake
whale
knows
hour
teacher

Across:

3. The friendly gray animal with the pointed nose that lives in the ocean
6. A compound word that means the trembling of the earth
8. The path of a spaceship as it circles the Earth
10. The animal with many sharp teeth that lives in the ocean

Down:

1. The largest mammal that lives in the ocean
2. A homophone for nose
3. A person who helps sick or hurt people
4. The compound word that means a hive for bees
5. A person who helps others learn
7. A homophone for our
9. A homophone for buy

Name: 

Homophone Match

Directions: Cut out the homophones cards on this page and the next page. Mix them up and lay them facedown. Turn over two cards at a time and try to find the matching homophones. When you get a pair, you keep them! The person with the most pairs, wins.

too	shone	eight	site
oar	sense	nose	fair
sew	new	which	wait
plain	pear	week	here
weak	threw	sore	for

Name: ______________________

know	some	shown	through
knew	two	no	pair
their	fare	ate	there
knows	sight	four	cents
plane	sum	weight	witch
hear	so	soar	or

Name: ____________________

Idioms

Idioms are a colorful way of saying something ordinary. The words in idioms do not mean exactly what they say.

Directions: Read the idioms listed below. Draw a picture of the literal meaning. Then match the idiom to its correct meaning.

Jump on the bandwagon! ●	● She doesn't eat very much.
She eats like a bird. ●	● Keep the secret.
Don't cry over spilled milk! ●	● Make sure you don't miss an opportunity
Don' t let the cat out of the bag! ●	● Get involved!
You are the apple of my eye. ●	● Don't worry about things that have already happened.
Don't miss the boat. ●	● I think you are special.

Name: ____________________

Poetry: Cinquains

A cinquain is a type of poetry. The form is:

Noun
Adjective, adjective
Verb + ing, verb + ing, verb + ing
Four-word phrase
Synonym for noun in line 1.

Example:

Books
Creative, fun
Reading, choosing, looking
I love to read!
Novels

Directions: Write your own cinquain!

____
noun

____________________, ____________________
adjective adjective

____________________, ____________________, ____________________
verb + ing verb + ing verb + ing

____
four-word phrase

____
synonym for noun in first line

Name: ____________________

Classifying

Classifying is putting similar things into categories or groups.

Directions: Write a word from the word box that describes the words in the sentence.

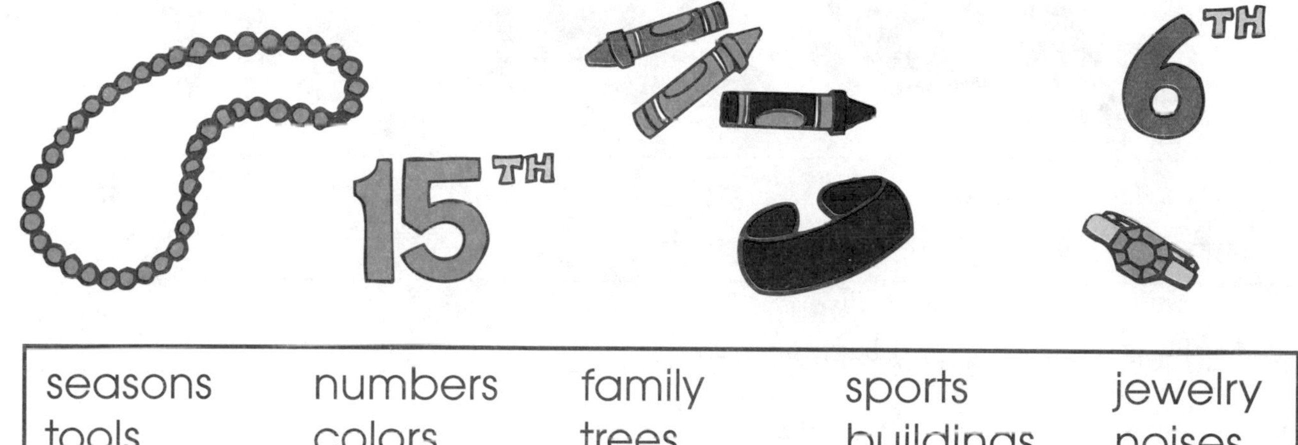

seasons	numbers	family	sports	jewelry
tools	colors	trees	buildings	noises

1. Maple, pine and oak are all names of ____________________.
2. Spring, summer, autumn and winter are the ____________________.
3. Sixth, ninth and fifteenth are all ____________________.
4. Saws, hammers and pliers are ____________________.
5. Aunt, parent and cousin are people in a ____________________.
6. Store, house and school are kinds of ____________________.
7. Green, purple and white are all ____________________.
8. Baseball, tennis and bowling are ____________________.
9. Necklace, pin and bracelet are ____________________.
10. Squeak, rattle and buzz are ____________________.

Name: ____________________

Classifying

Directions: Write the word from the word box that tells what kinds of things are in each sentence.

birds	toys	states	insects	women
men	numbers	animals	flowers	letters

1. A father, uncle and king are all ____________________.
2. Fred has a wagon, puzzles and blocks. These are all __________.
3. Iowa, Ohio and Maine are all ____________________.
4. A robin, woodpecker and canary all have wings. They are kinds of ____________________.
5. Squirrels, rabbits and foxes all have tails and are kinds of ____________________.
6. Roses, daisies and violets smell sweet. These are kinds of ____________________.
7. A, B, C and D are all __________. You use them to spell words.
8. Bees, ladybugs and beetles are kinds of ____________________.
9. Mother, aunt and queen are ____________________.
10. Seven, thirty and nineteen are all ____________________.

Name: ____________________

Classifying

Directions: After each sentence, write three words from the word box that belong.

eagle	whistle	horn	frog
dime	wheel	throat	ball
sun	airplane	penny	marble
banana	balloon	dollar	heart
camel	grasshopper	horse	kangaroo
chipmunk	lemon	butterfly	mouth

1. These are things that can hop.

   ____________ ____________ ____________

2. These things all have wings.

   ____________ ____________ ____________

3. These are types of money.

   ____________ ____________ ____________

4. These are four-legged animals.

   ____________ ____________ ____________

5. These are parts of your body.

   ____________ ____________ ____________

6. These things are yellow.

   ____________ ____________ ____________

7. These things can roll.

   ____________ ____________ ____________

8. These are things you can blow.

   ____________ ____________ ____________

Name: ____________________

Classifying

Directions: Look at the three words in each box and add one more that is like the others.

cars	trucks	cows	pigs
airplanes	________	chickens	________
bread	bagels	pens	pencils
muffins	________	paints	________
square	triangle	violets	tulips
rectangle	________	iris	________
milk	yogurt	mom	dad
cheese	________	sister	________
merry-go-round	swings	snowpants	boots
sandbox	________	jacket	________

Challenge: Can you list the theme of each group?

____________________ ____________________

____________________ ____________________

____________________ ____________________

____________________ ____________________

____________________ ____________________

Name: ____________________

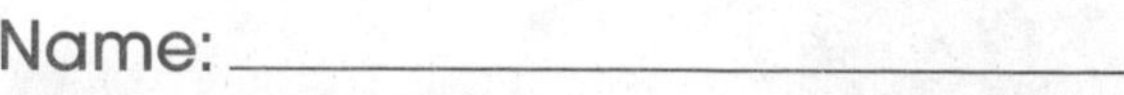

Classifying

Directions: In each box, circle the word that names the group the other words belong in. The first one is done for you.

cookies cakes (sweets) candy	shapes square circle triangle
diamond pearl ruby jewels	piano instruments drum horn
metals copper iron gold	lambs babies kittens puppies
door house floor window	pineapple coconut banana fruits
canary birds robin parrot	tiger jaguar lion cats
tree plants grass daffodil	coffee milk drinks juice
rain water steam ice	corn beans vegetables squash

Name: ____________________

Classifying

Directions: Write a word from the word box to complete each sentence. If the word you write names an article of clothing, write **1** on the line. If it names food, write **2** on the line. If it names an animal, write **3** on the line. If the word names furniture, write **4** on the line.

jacket	chair	shirt	owl	mice
bed	cheese	dress	bread	chocolate

__1__ 1. Danny tucked his ____________ into his pants.

_____ 2. ____________ is my favorite kind of candy.

_____ 3. The wise old ________ sat in the tree and said, "Who-o-o."

_____ 4. We can't sit on the ____________ because it has a broken leg.

_____ 5. Don't forget to wear your ____________ because it is chilly today.

_____ 6. Will you please buy a loaf of ____________ at the store?

_____ 7. She wore a very pretty ____________ to the dance.

_____ 8. The cat chased the ____________ in the barn.

_____ 9. I was so sleepy that I went to ____________ early.

_____ 10. We put ____________ in the mouse trap to help catch the mice.

Name: ______________________

Classifying

Directions: Write a word from the word box that is described by the four words in each group.

cake	farm	sick	winter	kite	car
flower	dishes	puppy	storm	ocean	book

leaves petals stem roots __________	sand shells waves fish __________	snow wind cold ice __________	string tail wind fly __________
fever headache pills sneeze __________	rain thunder wind hail __________	soft furry playful small __________	sugar butter flour chocolate __________
tractor animals barn plow __________	cup plate bowl platter __________	pages words pictures cover __________	tires seats windows trunk __________

Name: ____________________

Classifying

Directions: Write the word in each group that is the smallest, lowest or least amount. The first one is done for you.

1. toe, foot, body, leg ______toe______
2. dime, quarter, penny, nickel ____________
3. pour, drip, rain, sprinkle ____________
4. walk, skip, run, crawl ____________
5. bicycle, train, truck, car ____________
6. medium, large, tiny, huge ____________
7. stream, river, sea, ocean ____________
8. chimney, cellar, attic, roof ____________
9. canary, parrot, eagle, crow ____________
10. child, baby, adult, teenager ____________
11. roots, bark, branches, trunk ____________
12. pound, ton, ounce ____________
13. raft, steamship, motorboat, tugboat ____________
14. word, page, sentence, paragraph ____________
15. golf ball, tennis ball, football, basketball ____________

Name: 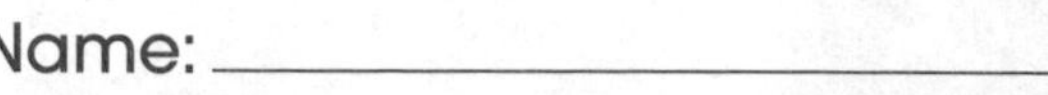

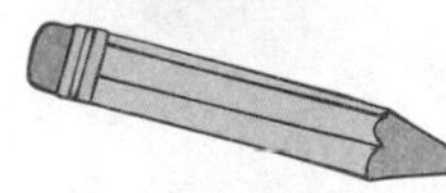

Classifying: School Word Find

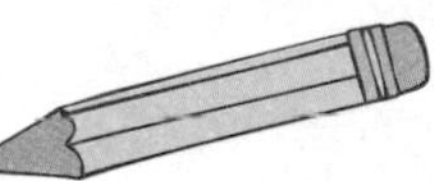

Directions: Look for the words located in the puzzle. Look forward, backward and diagonally.

p	e	n	z	c	e	c	h	a	l	k	i	f	m	o	p
a	e	r	u	l	e	r	e	r	e	l	p	a	t	s	u
p	b	n	y	m	n	a	c	g	b	l	a	r	a	k	z
e	v	o	c	d	l	y	r	a	n	o	i	t	c	i	d
r	i	k	q	i	d	o	q	r	s	p	n	x	a	b	e
j	x	w	v	h	l	n	u	s	e	w	t	c	l	f	s
b	o	o	k	s	o	s	t	d	u	i	s	g	c	n	k
m	k	j	n	f	z	t	e	r	l	s	t	y	u	v	s
o	p	k	c	o	l	c	r	q	g	u	n	m	l	o	p
c	h	a	l	k	b	o	a	r	d	f	j	w	a	r	u
h	a	l	z	e	x	g	s	s	e	l	p	a	t	s	w
a	g	y	n	b	a	d	e	c	h	i	l	j	o	e	k
c	o	m	p	u	t	e	r	t	a	l	u	c	r	a	c
s	c	i	s	s	o	r	s	k	o	o	b	e	t	o	n

paper	pencils	books	computer
scissors	crayons	erasers	chalkboard
ruler	dictionary	staples	clock
notebooks	stapler	desks	paints
pen	glue	chalk	calculator

Name: ____________________

Classifying: Seasons

Directions: Read each group of sentences. Decide which season is described in each group: winter, spring, summer or autumn. Draw a picture of that season.

I like to wear my boots. I also need to wear a coat. It is too cold to go swimming. It rains a lot and the snow melts. I like to play in the puddles and use my umbrella.

____

I have to wear boots and a coat. It is very cold outside. I like to make a snowman, then come inside for hot chocolate.

____

The leaves are changing color, and it is getting cooler. I go to school. I pick apples at the orchard with my family.

____

It is very hot. I go to the beach a lot. I also like to picnic outside. We watch fireworks.

____

Name: ____________________

Review

Directions: Read the story. Find words in the story that belong in the lists below. Write the words where they belong.

Tammy went on vacation with her father, mother and little sister, Beth. They planned to go to the beach for swimming, surfing and sailing. But on Tuesday, it rained. On Wednesday, it was too windy. On Thursday, it stormed. So Tammy and Beth stayed inside and played cards, checkers and marbles. They had a good time after all!

Family Words	Sports Words	Day Words
____________	____________	____________
____________	____________	____________
____________	____________	____________

Weather Words	Game Words
____________	____________
____________	____________
____________	____________

Name: ____________________

Webs

Webs are another way to classify information. Look at the groups below. Add more words in each group.

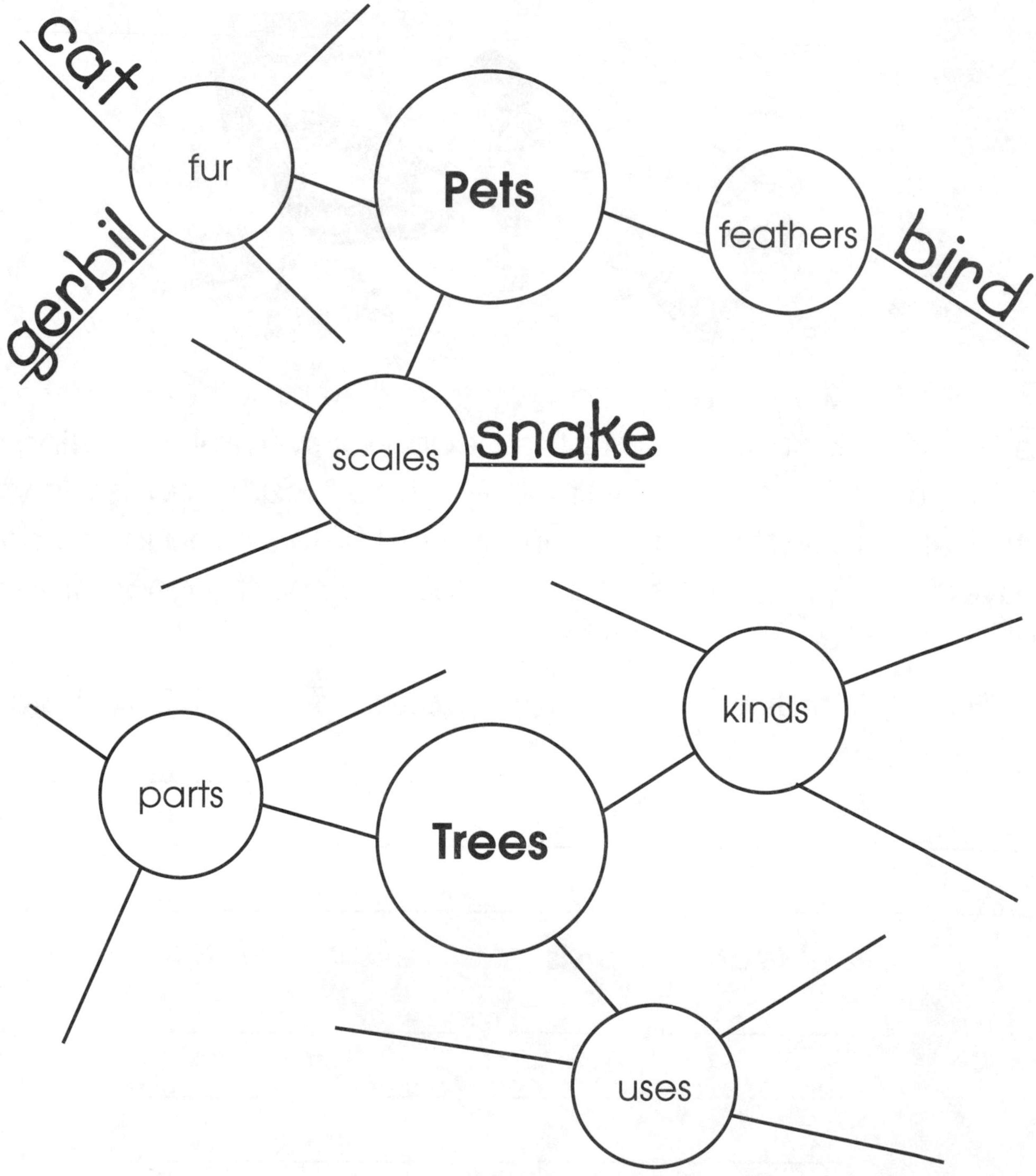

Pets
fur
cat
gerbil
feathers
bird
scales
snake

Trees
parts
kinds
uses

Name: ______________________

Story Webs

All short stories have a plot, characters, setting and a theme.

The **plot** is what the story is about.
The **characters** are the people or animals in the story.
The **setting** is where and when the story occurs.
The **theme** is the message or idea of the story.

Directions: Use the story "Snow White" to complete this story web.

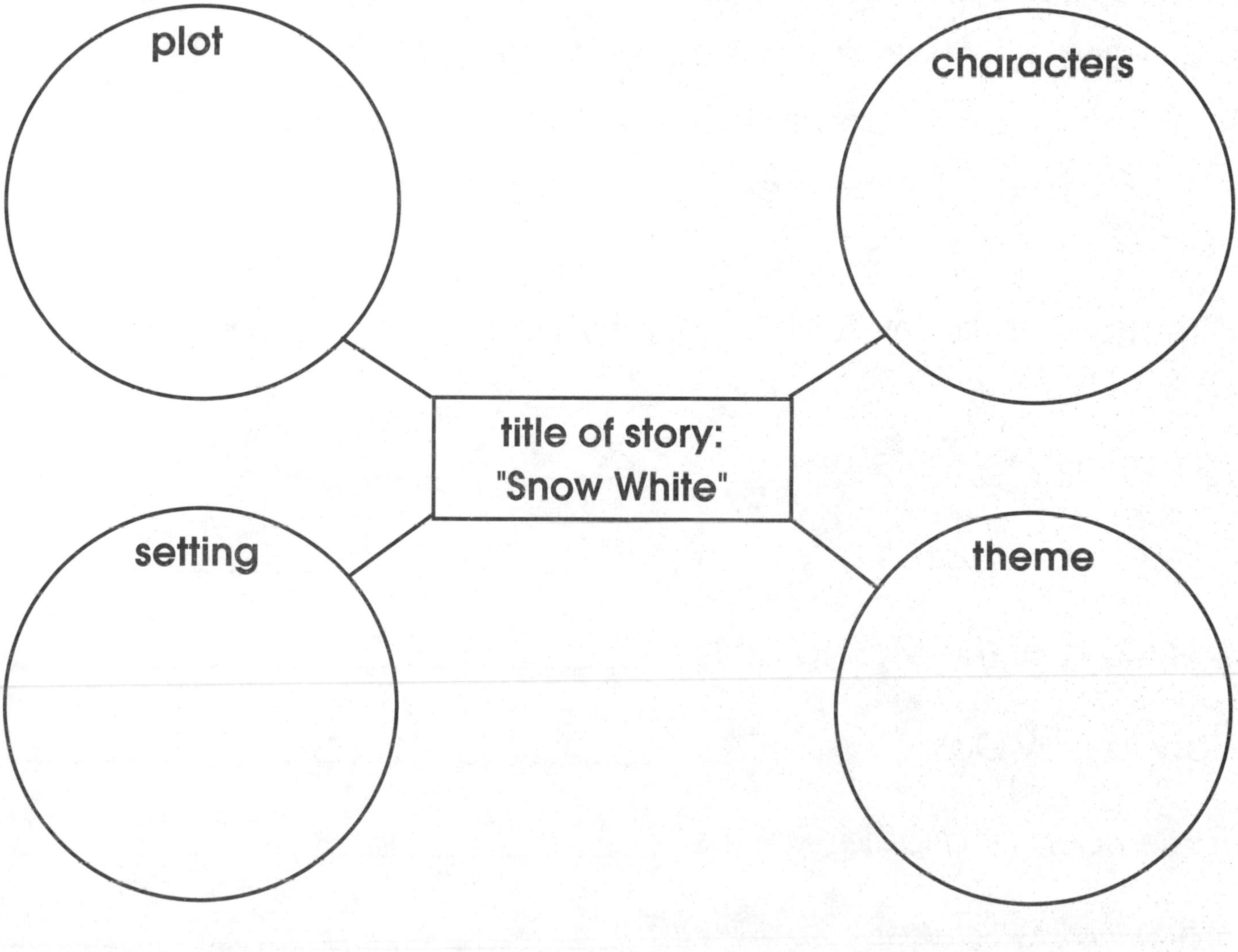

plot

characters

title of story:
"Snow White"

setting

theme

Name: ____________________

Types Of Books

A **fiction** book is a book about things that are made up or not true. Fantasy books are fiction. A **nonfiction** book is about things that have really happened. Books can be classified into more types:

Mystery - books that have clues that lead to solving a problem or mystery

Biography - book about a real person's life

Poetry - a collection of poems, which may or may not rhyme

Fantasy - books about things that cannot really happen

Sports - books about different sports or sport figures

Travel - books about going to other places

Directions: Write mystery, biography, poetry, fantasy, sports or travel next to each title.

The Life of Helen Keller ____________________

Let's Go to Mexico! ____________________

The Case of the Missing Doll ____________________

How to Play Golf ____________________

Turtle Soup and Other Poems ____________________

Fred's Flying Saucer ____________________

Name: ____________________

Types of Books: Fiction and Nonfiction

Directions: Cut out the titles and place them in the correct category.

Fiction	Nonfiction

cut ✂ -

The Three Little Pigs	How to Grow a Garden
All About Trees	The Life of George Washington
Spaceboy Sammy	Jack and the Beanstalk
Curious George	Farm Life
Arts and Crafts	Little Red Riding Hood

Page is blank for cutting exercise on previous page.

Name: 

Bookmarks

Bookmarks help to keep our place in the books we are reading, so we can find it later. Make two bookmarks to use in your favorite books

Directions: Color the two bookmarks and cut them out.

Name: ______________________

Review: My Reading Alphabet

Directions: Use the terms you have learned to create an alphabet of reading words! Here are a few to get you started.

A

B

Characters

D

E

Fiction

G

H

I

J

K

L

Mysteries

N

O

P

Q

R

S

T

U

V

Words

X

Y

Z

GLOSSARY

Biography: A type of nonfiction book written about a real person's life.

Classifying: Putting similar things into categories or groups.

Compound Words: Two words which are put together to make one new word. Example: **sandbox**.

Consonants: Letters that are not vowels (every letter except a, e, i, o and u).

Cinquain: A five-line poem that follows the following form:

Line 1: noun
Line 2: adjective, adjective
Line 3: verb + ing, verb + ing, verb + ing
Line 4: four-word phrase
Line 5: synonym for noun in line 1.

Fiction: A type of book about things that are made up or not true.

Homophones: Two words that sound the same, but have different meanings and are usually spelled differently. Example: **write** and **right**.

Idiom: A saying in which the words do not mean exactly what they say.

Inference: Using logic to figure out what is not directly told.

Main Idea: Finding the most important points. The main idea is what the story is mostly about.

Nonfiction: A type of book about things that have really happened.

Phonics: Using the sound letters make to decode unknown words.

Rhymes: Words with the same ending sounds. Example: **lake** and **cake**.

Riddles: A puzzling question. Clues are usually provided to solve riddles.

Syllable: Word parts. Each syllable has one vowel sound.

Syllabication: Dividing words into parts, each with a vowel sound.

Synonyms: Words that mean the same or nearly the same thing.

Answer Key

Master Skills Reading 3

Name: ____________

My Story

Directions: Fill in the blanks. Use these sentences to write a story about yourself.

Answers will vary.

I feel happy when ____________.

I feel sad when ____________.

I am good at ____________.

Words that describe me: ____________ ____________ ____________ ____________ ____________

I can help at home by ____________.

My friends like me because ____________.

I like to ____________.

My favorite food is ____________.

My favorite animal is ____________.

Now . . . take your answers and write a story about **you**!

2

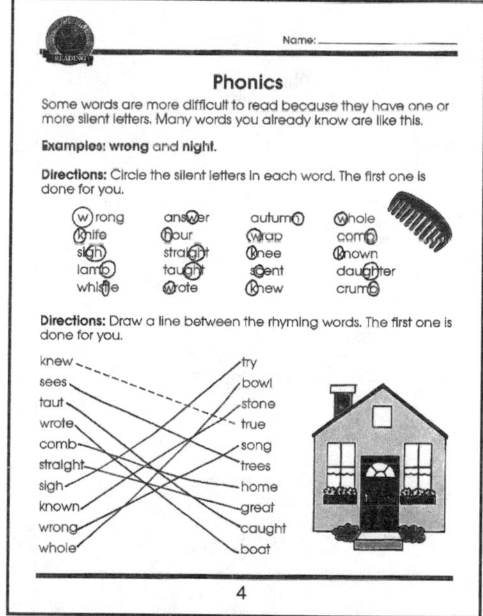

Name: ____________

Phonics

Some words are more difficult to read because they have one or more silent letters. Many words you already know are like this.

Examples: wrong and **night**.

Directions: Circle the silent letters in each word. The first one is done for you.

wrong	answer	autumn	whole
knife	hour	wrap	comb
sigh	straight	knee	known
lamb	taught	scent	daughter
whistle	wrote	knew	crumb

Directions: Draw a line between the rhyming words. The first one is done for you.

knew	try
sees	bowl
taut	stone
wrote	true
comb	song
straight	trees
sigh	home
known	great
wrong	caught
whole	boat

4

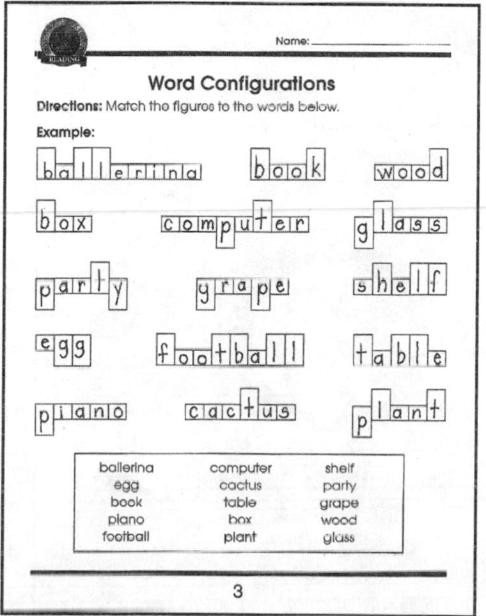

Name: ____________

Word Configurations

Directions: Match the figures to the words below.

Example:

ballerina book wood

box computer glass

party grape shelf

egg football table

piano cactus plant

ballerina	computer	shelf
egg	cactus	party
book	table	grape
piano	box	wood
football	plant	glass

3

Name: ____________

Phonics

Sometimes letters make sounds you don't expect. Two consonants can work together to make the sound of one consonant. The **f** sound can be made by **ph**, as in the word **elephant**. The consonants **gh** are most often silent, as in the words **night** and **though**. But they also can make the **f** sound as in the word **laugh**.

Directions: Circle the letters that make the **f** sound. Write the correct word from the box to complete each sentence.

elephant	cough	laugh	telephone	phonics
dolphins	enough	tough	alphabet	rough

1. The **dolphins** were playing in the sea.
2. Did you have enough time to do your homework?
3. A cold can make you cough and sneeze.
4. The elephant ate peanuts with his trunk.
5. The road to my school is rough and bumpy.
6. You had a telephone call this morning.
7. The tough meat was hard to chew.
8. Studying phonics will help you read better.
9. The alphabet has 26 letters in it.
10. We began to laugh when the clowns came in.

5

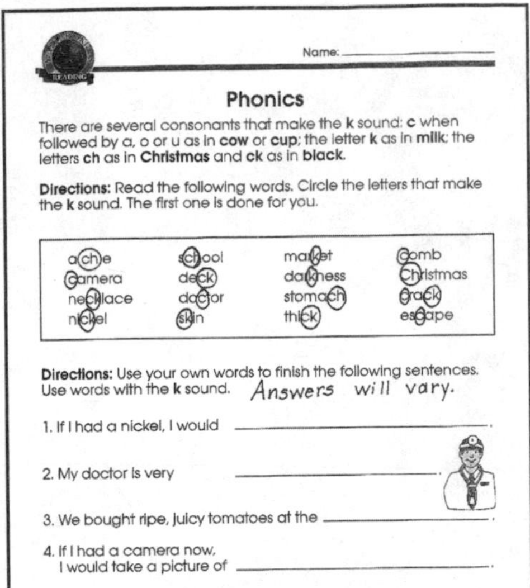

Name: __________

Phonics

There are several consonants that make the **k** sound: **c** when followed by a, o or u as in **cow** or **cup**; the letter **k** as in **milk**; the letters **ch** as in **Christmas** and **ck** as in **black**.

Directions: Read the following words. Circle the letters that make the **k** sound. The first one is done for you.

ache	school	market	comb
camera	deck	darkness	Christmas
necklace	doctor	stomach	crack
nickel	skin	thick	escape

Directions: Use your own words to finish the following sentences. Use words with the **k** sound. *Answers will vary.*

1. If I had a nickel, I would __________.
2. My doctor is very __________.
3. We bought ripe, juicy tomatoes at the __________.
4. If I had a camera now, I would take a picture of __________.
5. When my stomach aches, __________.

6

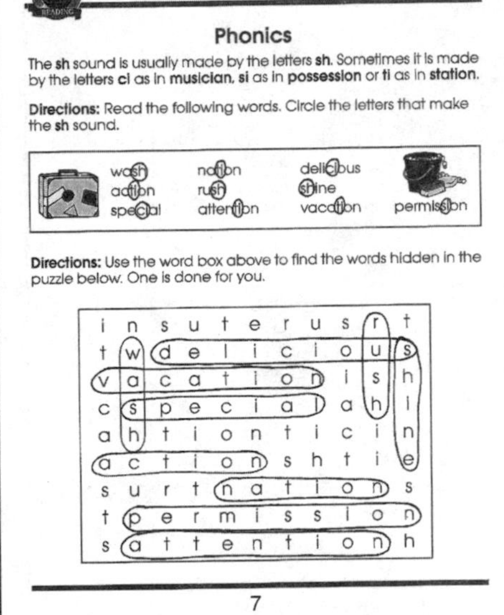

Name: __________

Phonics

The **sh** sound is usually made by the letters **sh**. Sometimes it is made by the letters **ci** as in **musician**, **si** as in **possession** or **ti** as in **station**.

Directions: Read the following words. Circle the letters that make the **sh** sound.

wash	nation	delicious	
action	rush	shine	
special	attention	vacation	permission

Directions: Use the word box above to find the words hidden in the puzzle below. One is done for you.

i	n	s	u	t	e	r	u	s	r	t
t	w	d	e	l	i	c	i	o	u	s
v	a	c	a	t	i	o	n	i	s	h
c	s	p	e	c	i	a	l	a	h	i
a	h	t	i	o	n	t	i	c	i	n
a	c	t	i	o	n	s	h	t	i	e
s	u	r	t	n	a	t	i	o	n	s
t	p	e	r	m	i	s	s	i	o	n
s	a	t	t	e	n	t	i	o	n	h

7

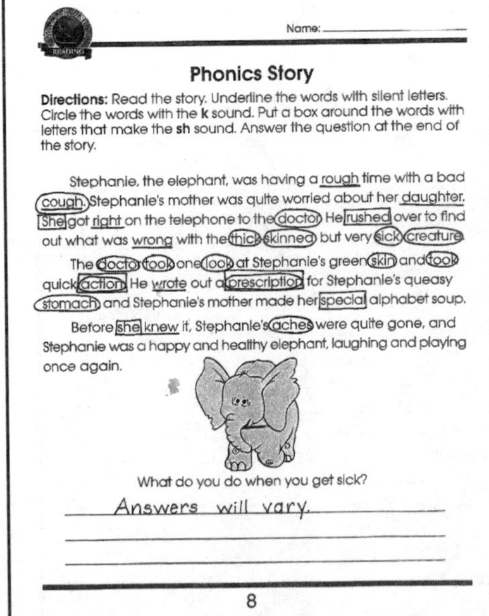

Name: __________

Phonics Story

Directions: Read the story. Underline the words with silent letters. Circle the words with the **k** sound. Put a box around the words with letters that make the **sh** sound. Answer the question at the end of the story.

Stephanie, the elephant, was having a rough time with a bad cough. Stephanie's mother was quite worried about her daughter. She got right on the telephone to the doctor. He rushed over to find out what was wrong with the thick-skinned but very sick creature.

The doctor took one look at Stephanie's green skin and took quick action. He wrote out a prescription for Stephanie's queasy stomach and Stephanie's mother made her special alphabet soup.

Before she knew it, Stephanie's aches were quite gone, and Stephanie was a happy and healthy elephant, laughing and playing once again.

What do you do when you get sick?

Answers will vary.

8

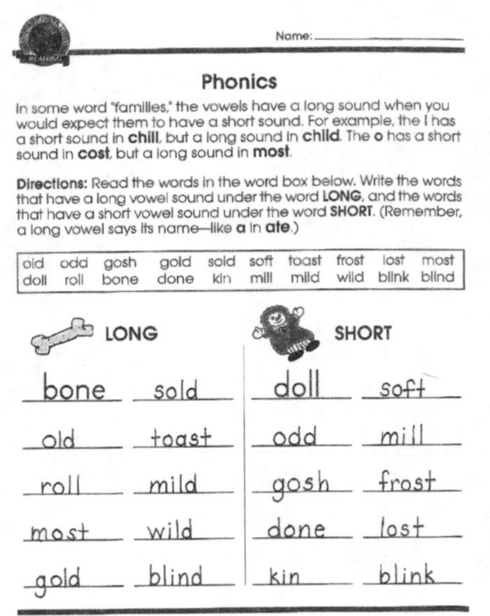

Name: __________

Phonics

In some word "families," the vowels have a long sound when you would expect them to have a short sound. For example, the **i** has a short sound in **chill**, but a long sound in **child**. The **o** has a short sound in **cost**, but a long sound in **most**.

Directions: Read the words in the word box below. Write the words that have a long vowel sound under the word **LONG**, and the words that have a short vowel sound under the word **SHORT**. (Remember, a long vowel says its name—like **a** in **ate**.)

old	odd	gosh	gold	sold	soft	toast	frost	lost	most
doll	roll	bone	done	kin	mill	mild	wild	blink	blind

LONG		SHORT	
bone	sold	doll	soft
old	toast	odd	mill
roll	mild	gosh	frost
most	wild	done	lost
gold	blind	kin	blink

9

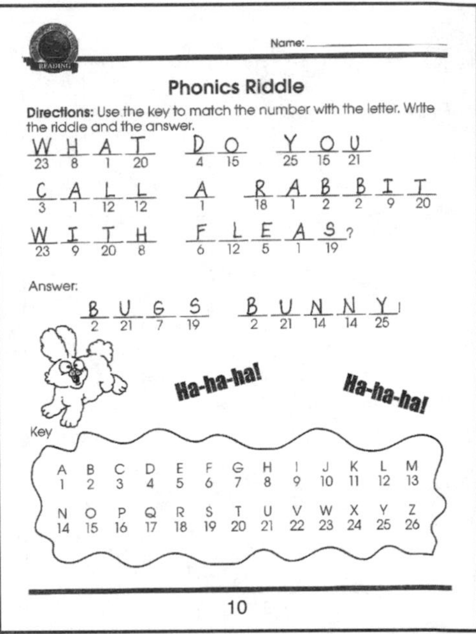

Name: __________

Phonics Riddle

Directions: Use the key to match the number with the letter. Write the riddle and the answer.

W H A T (23 8 1 20) D O (4 15) Y O U (25 15 21)
C A L L (3 1 12 12) A (1) R A B B I T (18 1 2 2 9 20)
W I T H (23 9 20 8) F L E A S (6 12 5 1 19)?

Answer: B U G S (2 21 7 19) B U N N Y (2 21 14 14 25)

Ha-ha-ha! Ha-ha-ha!

Key

A	B	C	D	E	F	G	H	I	J	K	L	M
1	2	3	4	5	6	7	8	9	10	11	12	13
N	**O**	**P**	**Q**	**R**	**S**	**T**	**U**	**V**	**W**	**X**	**Y**	**Z**
14	15	16	17	18	19	20	21	22	23	24	25	26

10

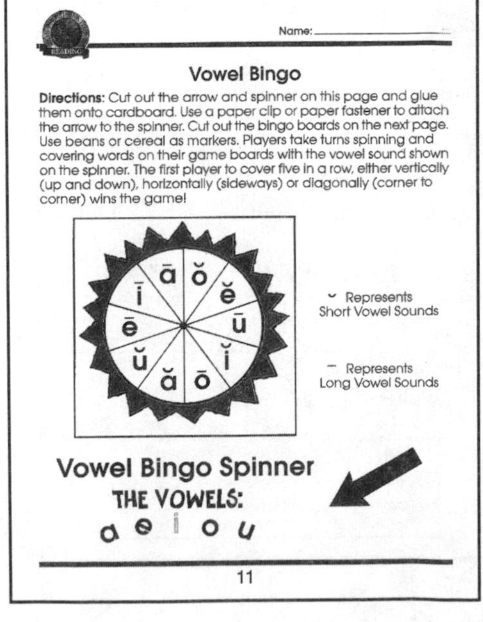

Name: __________

Vowel Bingo

Directions: Cut out the arrow and spinner on this page and glue them onto cardboard. Use a paper clip or paper fastener to attach the arrow to the spinner. Cut out the bingo boards on the next page. Use beans or cereal as markers. Players take turns spinning and covering words on their game boards with the vowel sound shown on the spinner. The first player to cover five in a row, either vertically (up and down), horizontally (sideways) or diagonally (corner to corner) wins the game!

˘ Represents Short Vowel Sounds

¯ Represents Long Vowel Sounds

Vowel Bingo Spinner

THE VOWELS: a e i o u

11

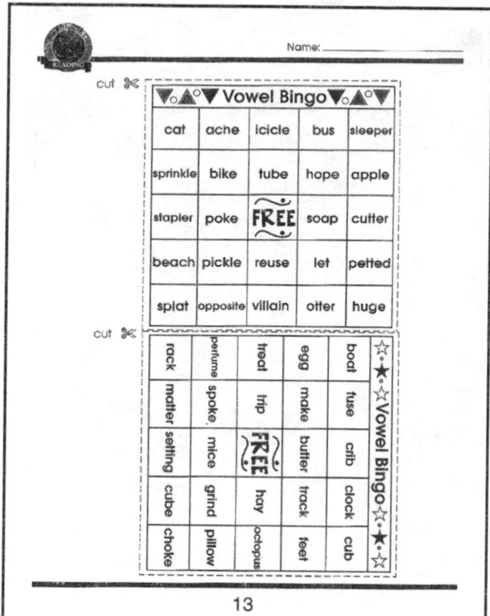

Name: ______

cut ✂

Vowel Bingo

cat	ache	icicle	bus	sleeper
sprinkle	bike	tube	hope	apple
stapler	poke	FREE	soap	cutter
beach	pickle	reuse	let	petted
splat	opposite	villain	otter	huge

cut ✂

Vowel Bingo

boat	fuse	crib	clock	cub
egg	make	butter	track	feet
treat	trip	FREE	hay	octopus
perfume	spoke	mice	grind	pillow
rack	matter	setting	cube	choke

13

Name: ______

Phonics

Sometimes, vowels have unusual sounds that are neither short nor long. For example, often when an **a** is followed by an **l**, instead of the short **a** sound, as in **apple**, it has the sound in **ball**. Sometimes an **o** has the sound of short **u**, as in **done**.

Directions: Read the words in the following word "families." Write another word in each group.

The **al** and **all** families: also, always, ball, small, tall, ______ *Answers will vary.*

The **alk** family: chalk, stalk, talk, ______

The **alt** family: halt, malt, ______

The **o** family: done, come, other, ______

Directions: Draw lines to match the rhyming words.

glove	call
pull	halt
wall	shove
salt	talk
walk	full

15

Name: ______

Syllables

All words can be divided into **syllables**. Syllables are word parts which have one vowel sound in each part.

Directions: Draw a line between the syllable part and write the word on the correct line below. The first one is done for you.

lit|tle, truck, pen|cil, re|joic|ing, bum|ble|bee, daz|zle, flag, ant, pil|low, dog, an|gel|ic, tel|e|phone

1 SYLLABLE	2 SYLLABLES	3 SYLLABLES
truck	little	rejoicing
flag	pencil	bumblebee
ant	dazzle	angelic
dog	pillow	telephone

16

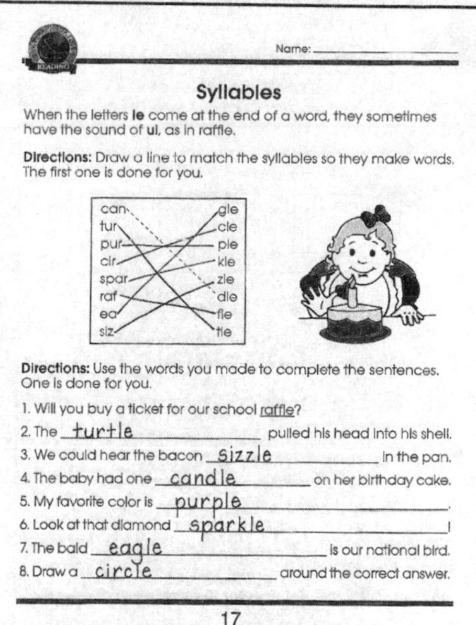

Name: ______

Syllables

When the letters **le** come at the end of a word, they sometimes have the sound of **ul**, as in raffle.

Directions: Draw a line to match the syllables so they make words. The first one is done for you.

can	gle
tur	cle
pur	ple
cir	kle
spar	zle
raf	dle
ea	fle
siz	tle

Directions: Use the words you made to complete the sentences. One is done for you.

1. Will you buy a ticket for our school raffle?
2. The *turtle* pulled his head into his shell.
3. We could hear the bacon *sizzle* in the pan.
4. The baby had one *candle* on her birthday cake.
5. My favorite color is *purple*.
6. Look at that diamond *sparkle*!
7. The bald *eagle* is our national bird.
8. Draw a *circle* around the correct answer.

17

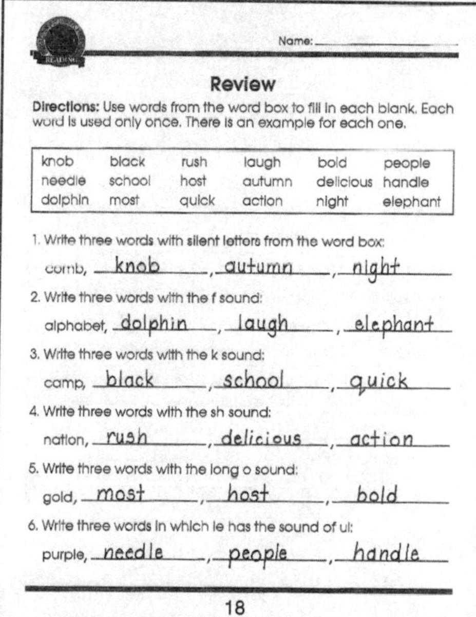

Name: ______

Review

Directions: Use words from the word box to fill in each blank. Each word is used only once. There is an example for each one.

knob	black	rush	laugh	bold	people
needle	school	host	autumn	delicious	handle
dolphin	most	quick	action	night	elephant

1. Write three words with silent letters from the word box: comb, *knob*, *autumn*, *night*
2. Write three words with the f sound: alphabet, *dolphin*, *laugh*, *elephant*
3. Write three words with the k sound: camp, *black*, *school*, *quick*
4. Write three words with the sh sound: nation, *rush*, *delicious*, *action*
5. Write three words with the long o sound: gold, *most*, *host*, *bold*
6. Write three words in which le has the sound of ul: purple, *needle*, *people*, *handle*

18

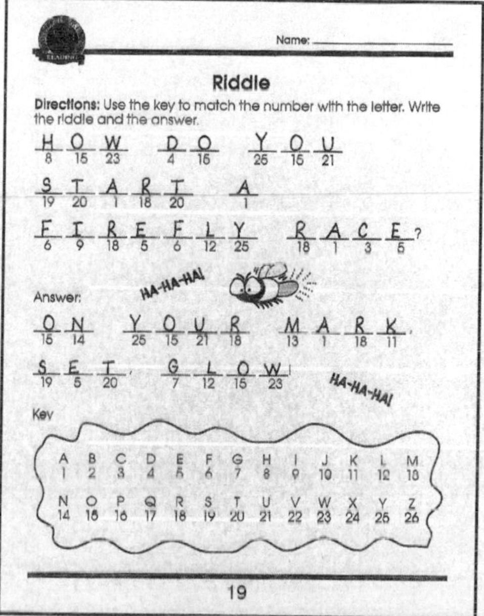

Name: ______

Riddle

Directions: Use the key to match the number with the letter. Write the riddle and the answer.

H O W D O Y O U S T A R T A F I R E F L Y R A C E?
8 15 23 4 15 25 15 21 19 20 1 18 20 1 6 9 18 5 6 12 25 18 1 3 5

Answer: O N Y O U R M A R K, S E T, G L O W!
15 14 25 15 21 18 13 1 18 11 19 5 20 7 12 15 23

Key

A	B	C	D	E	F	G	H	I	J	K	L	M
1	2	3	4	5	6	7	8	9	10	11	12	13

N	O	P	Q	R	S	T	U	V	W	X	Y	Z
14	15	16	17	18	19	20	21	22	23	24	25	26

19

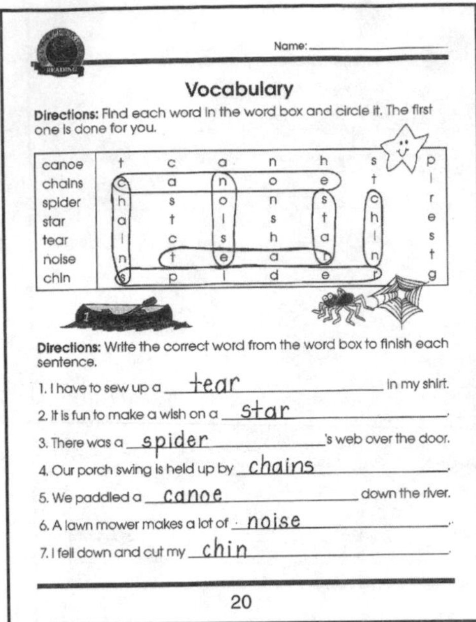

Name: ______

Vocabulary

Directions: Find each word in the word box and circle it. The first one is done for you.

canoe	t	c	a	n	h	s	p
chains	c	a	n	o	e	t	l
spider	h	s	o	n	s	c	r
star	a	t	l	s	t	h	e
tear	i	c	s	h	a	i	s
noise	n	t	e	a	r	n	t
chin	s	p	i	d	e	r	g

Directions: Write the correct word from the word box to finish each sentence.

1. I have to sew up a tear in my shirt.
2. It is fun to make a wish on a star.
3. There was a spider's web over the door.
4. Our porch swing is held up by chains.
5. We paddled a canoe down the river.
6. A lawn mower makes a lot of noise.
7. I fell down and cut my chin.

20

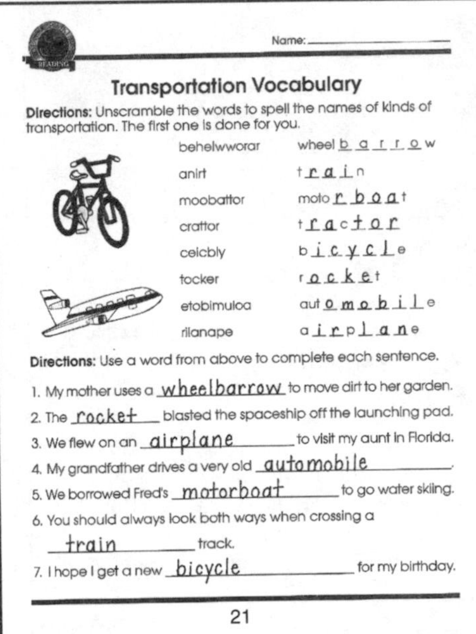

Name: ______

Transportation Vocabulary

Directions: Unscramble the words to spell the names of kinds of transportation. The first one is done for you.

behelwworar — wheelbarrow
anirt — train
moobattor — motorboat
crattor — tractor
celcbly — bicycle
tocker — rocket
etobimuloa — automobile
rilanape — airplane

Directions: Use a word from above to complete each sentence.

1. My mother uses a wheelbarrow to move dirt to her garden.
2. The rocket blasted the spaceship off the launching pad.
3. We flew on an airplane to visit my aunt in Florida.
4. My grandfather drives a very old automobile.
5. We borrowed Fred's motorboat to go water skiing.
6. You should always look both ways when crossing a train track.
7. I hope I get a new bicycle for my birthday.

21

Name: ______

Cooking Tools Vocabulary

Directions: Unscramble the words to spell the names of things you use when you cook. The first one is done for you.

mlwrcovae microwave
easmrlugn spuc measuring cups
imrxe mixer
stop pots
pnas pans
ponoss spoons
veon oven
mrtie timer
tsla nad pppeer salt and pepper
wlbos bowls

What is your favorite recipe?
Answers will vary.

22

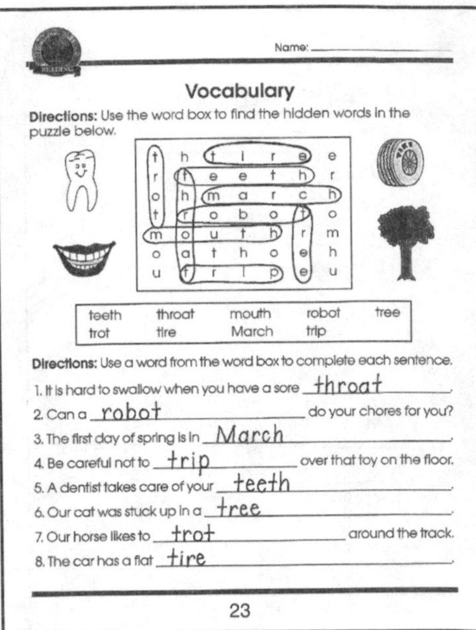

Name: ______

Vocabulary

Directions: Use the word box to find the hidden words in the puzzle below.

t	h	t	i	r	e	e
r	t	e	e	t	h	r
o	h	m	a	r	c	h
t	r	o	b	o	t	o
m	o	u	t	h	r	m
o	a	t	h	o	e	h
u	t	r	i	p	e	u

teeth throat mouth robot tree
trot tire March trip

Directions: Use a word from the word box to complete each sentence.

1. It is hard to swallow when you have a sore throat.
2. Can a robot do your chores for you?
3. The first day of spring is in March.
4. Be careful not to trip over that toy on the floor.
5. A dentist takes care of your teeth.
6. Our cat was stuck up in a tree.
7. Our horse likes to trot around the track.
8. The car has a flat tire.

23

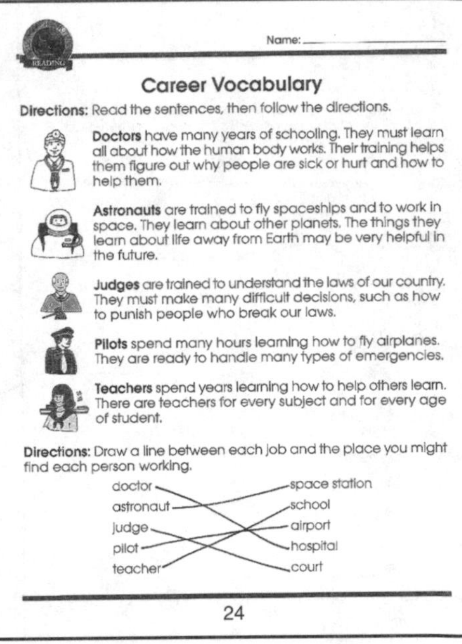

Name: ______

Career Vocabulary

Directions: Read the sentences, then follow the directions.

Doctors have many years of schooling. They must learn all about how the human body works. Their training helps them figure out why people are sick or hurt and how to help them.

Astronauts are trained to fly spaceships and to work in space. They learn about other planets. The things they learn about life away from Earth may be very helpful in the future.

Judges are trained to understand the laws of our country. They must make many difficult decisions, such as how to punish people who break our laws.

Pilots spend many hours learning how to fly airplanes. They are ready to handle many types of emergencies.

Teachers spend years learning how to help others learn. There are teachers for every subject and for every age of student.

Directions: Draw a line between each job and the place you might find each person working.

doctor — hospital
astronaut — space station
judge — court
pilot — airport
teacher — school

24

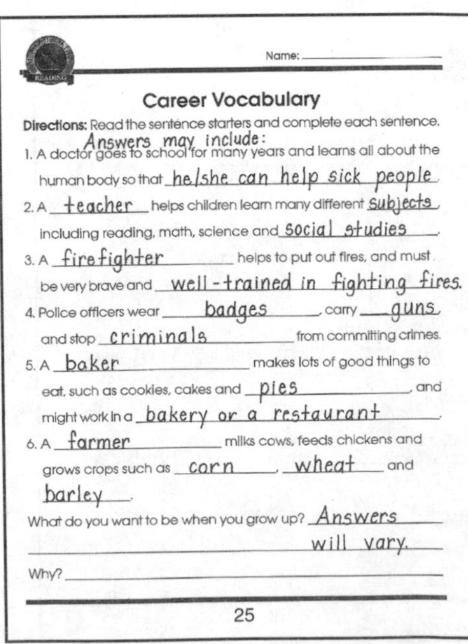

Name: ______

Career Vocabulary

Directions: Read the sentence starters and complete each sentence.

Answers may include:

1. A doctor goes to school for many years and learns all about the human body so that he/she can help sick people.
2. A teacher helps children learn many different subjects, including reading, math, science and social studies.
3. A firefighter helps to put out fires, and must be very brave and well-trained in fighting fires.
4. Police officers wear badges, carry guns, and stop criminals from committing crimes.
5. A baker makes lots of good things to eat, such as cookies, cakes and pies, and might work in a bakery or a restaurant.
6. A farmer milks cows, feeds chickens and grows crops such as corn, wheat and barley.

What do you want to be when you grow up? Answers will vary.

Why? ______

25

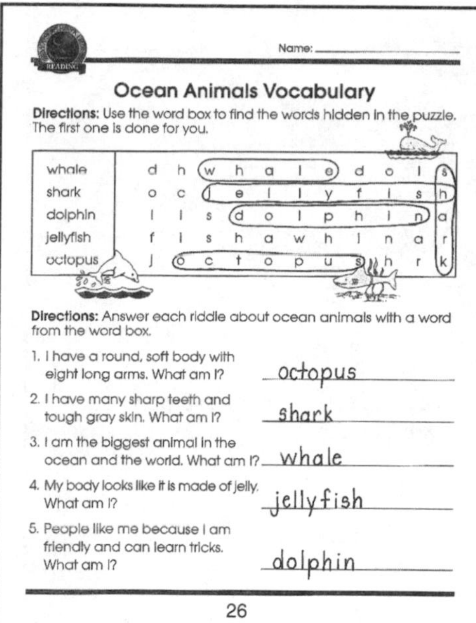

Name: ____________

Ocean Animals Vocabulary

Directions: Use the word box to find the words hidden in the puzzle. The first one is done for you.

Word box	Puzzle
whale	d h w h a l e d o l s
shark	o c j e l l y f i s h
dolphin	l i s d o l p h i n a
jellyfish	f i s h a w h i n a r
octopus	j o c t o p u s h r k

Directions: Answer each riddle about ocean animals with a word from the word box.

1. I have a round, soft body with eight long arms. What am I? octopus
2. I have many sharp teeth and tough gray skin. What am I? shark
3. I am the biggest animal in the ocean and the world. What am I? whale
4. My body looks like it is made of jelly. What am I? jellyfish
5. People like me because I am friendly and can learn tricks. What am I? dolphin

26

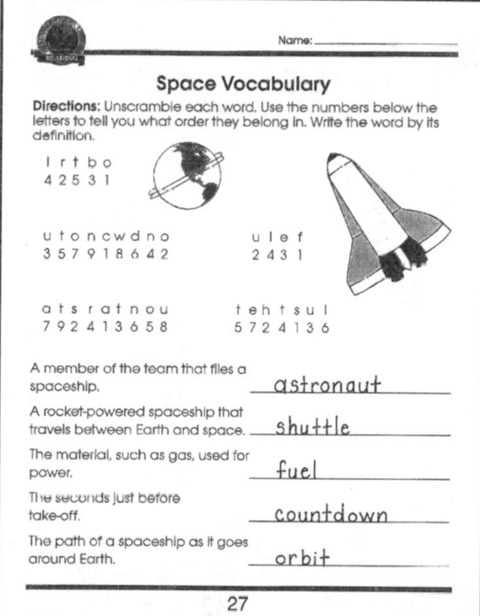

Name: ____________

Space Vocabulary

Directions: Unscramble each word. Use the numbers below the letters to tell you what order they belong in. Write the word by its definition.

l r t b o
4 2 5 3 1

u t o n c w d n o
3 5 7 9 1 8 6 4 2

u l e f
2 4 3 1

a t s r a t n o u
7 9 2 4 1 3 6 5 8

t e h t s u l
5 7 2 4 1 3 6

A member of the team that flies a spaceship. astronaut

A rocket-powered spaceship that travels between Earth and space. shuttle

The material, such as gas, used for power. fuel

The seconds just before take-off. countdown

The path of a spaceship as it goes around Earth. orbit

27

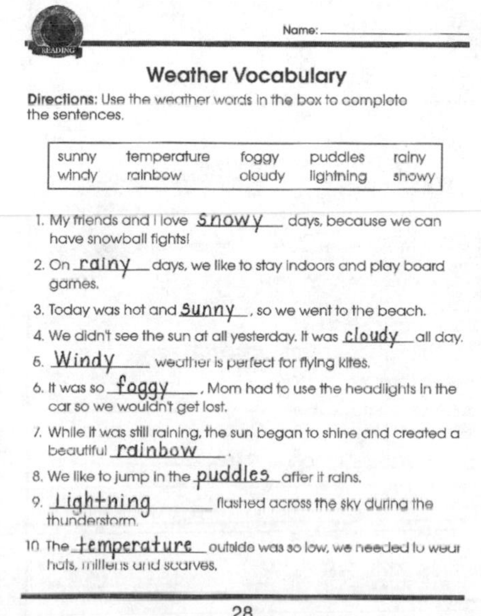

Name: ____________

Weather Vocabulary

Directions: Use the weather words in the box to complete the sentences.

sunny	temperature	foggy	puddles	rainy
windy	rainbow	cloudy	lightning	snowy

1. My friends and I love snowy days, because we can have snowball fights!
2. On rainy days, we like to stay indoors and play board games.
3. Today was hot and sunny, so we went to the beach.
4. We didn't see the sun at all yesterday. It was cloudy all day.
5. Windy weather is perfect for flying kites.
6. It was so foggy, Mom had to use the headlights in the car so we wouldn't get lost.
7. While it was still raining, the sun began to shine and created a beautiful rainbow.
8. We like to jump in the puddles after it rains.
9. Lightning flashed across the sky during the thunderstorm.
10. The temperature outside was so low, we needed to wear hats, mittens and scarves.

28

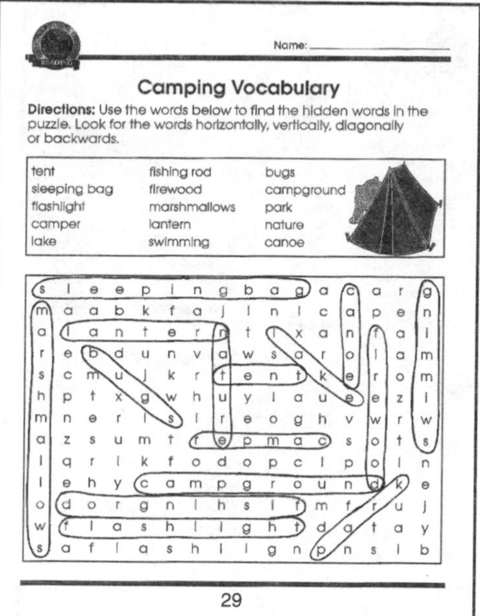

Name: ____________

Camping Vocabulary

Directions: Use the words below to find the hidden words in the puzzle. Look for the words horizontally, vertically, diagonally or backwards.

tent	fishing rod	bugs
sleeping bag	firewood	campground
flashlight	marshmallows	park
camper	lantern	nature
lake	swimming	canoe

s l e e p i n g b a g a c a r g
m a a b k f a j l n l c a p e n
a l a n t e r n t l x a n f a l
r e b d u n v a w s a r o l a m
s c m u j k r t e n t k e r o m
h p t x g w h u y l a u e e z l
m n e r l s l r e o g h v w r w
a z s u m t r e p m a c s o t s
l q r l k f o d o p c l p o l n
l e h y c a m p g r o u n d k e
o d o r g n l h s l f m f r u j
w f l a s h l i g h t d a t a y
s a f l a s h l i g n p n s l b

29

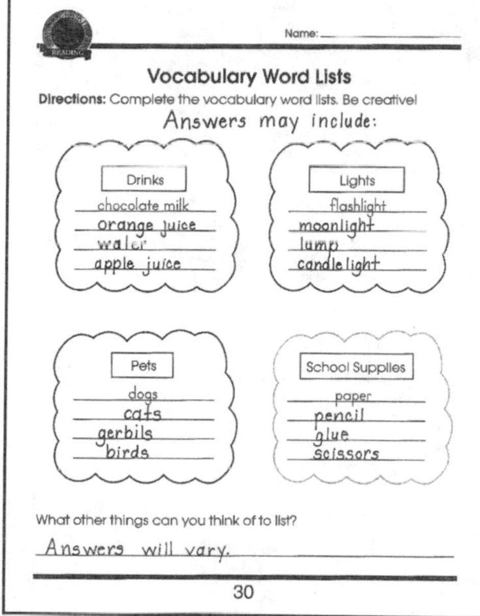

Name: ____________

Vocabulary Word Lists

Directions: Complete the vocabulary word lists. Be creative!

Answers may include:

Drinks: chocolate milk, orange juice, water, apple juice

Lights: flashlight, moonlight, lamp, candle light

Pets: dogs, cats, gerbils, birds

School Supplies: paper, pencil, glue, scissors

What other things can you think of to list? Answers will vary.

30

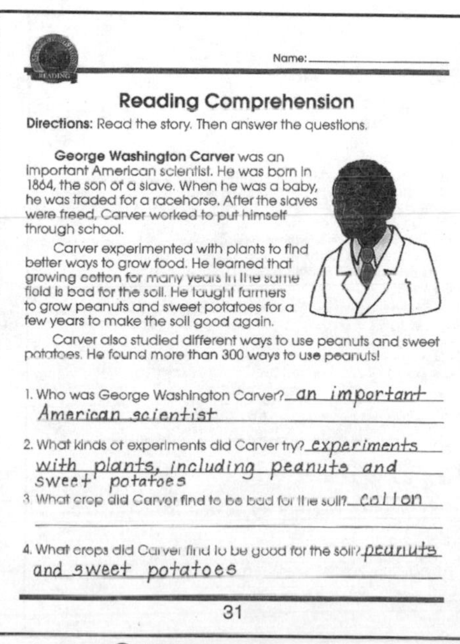

Name: ____________

Reading Comprehension

Directions: Read the story. Then answer the questions.

George Washington Carver was an important American scientist. He was born in 1864, the son of a slave. When he was a baby, he was traded for a racehorse. After the slaves were freed, Carver worked to put himself through school.

Carver experimented with plants to find better ways to grow food. He learned that growing cotton for many years in the same field is bad for the soil. He taught farmers to grow peanuts and sweet potatoes for a few years to make the soil good again.

Carver also studied different ways to use peanuts and sweet potatoes. He found more than 300 ways to use peanuts!

1. Who was George Washington Carver? an important American scientist
2. What kinds of experiments did Carver try? experiments with plants, including peanuts and sweet potatoes
3. What crop did Carver find to be bad for the soil? cotton
4. What crops did Carver find to be good for the soil? peanuts and sweet potatoes

31

Name: ____________

Reading Comprehension

Directions: Read the story. Then answer the questions.

You can grow a **citrus** (SIT-russ) plant in your home. Citrus fruits include lemons, oranges and grapefruits. Collect seeds from a piece of fruit. Wash the seeds with water and let them dry for three days. Next, fill a four-inch pot with potting soil. You can buy soil at a garden store. Plant the seeds about one-inch deep and water thoroughly.

Plants need water and light to grow. Put your pot near a window where it can get light from the sun. Pour a little water on the soil after you plant the seeds. When the soil feels dry, water it again.

1. What are some kinds of citrus fruits? lemons, oranges and grapefruits
2. How deep should you plant the seeds in the soil? one-inch deep
3. Name two things that plants need to grow.
   1) water 2) light
4. How do you know when to water your plant? when the soil feels dry.

32

Name: ____________

Reading Comprehension

Directions: Read the story. Then answer the questions.

Weed is the word used for any plant that grows where it is not wanted. Grasses that grow in your flower or vegetable garden are weeds. An unwanted flower growing in your lawn is also a weed. Dandelions are this kind of weed.

People do not plant weeds. They grow very fast. If you do not pull them out or kill them, weeds will crowd out the plants that you want to grow. The seeds of many kinds of weeds are spread by the wind. Birds and other animals also carry weed seeds.

1. A weed is any plant that grows where it is not wanted.
2. One kind of flowering weed is the dandelion
3. Two things that spread the seeds of weeds are wind and birds and other animals.

33

Name: ____________

Reading Comprehension

Directions: Read the story. Then answer the questions.

What is a **robot**? Does a robot do any of your work for you?

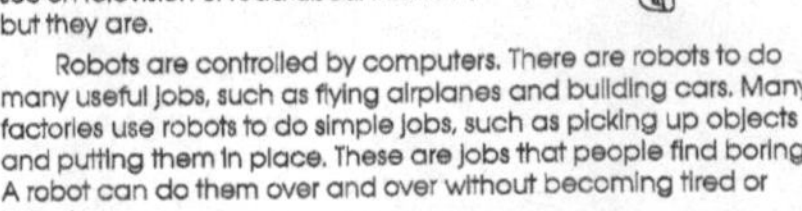

A robot is any machine that can do work without a person being needed to run it all the time. A dishwasher is a kind of robot. A clock radio is a robot, too. They may not look like the robots you see on television or read about in books, but they are.

Robots are controlled by computers. There are robots to do many useful jobs, such as flying airplanes and building cars. Many factories use robots to do simple jobs, such as picking up objects and putting them in place. These are jobs that people find boring. A robot can do them over and over without becoming tired or bored.

1. What is a robot? Any machine that can do work without a person running it all the time.
2. Name two uses for robots.
   1) flying airplanes 2) building cars
3. What controls a robot? computers

34

Name: ____________

Reading Comprehension

Directions: Read the story. Then answer the questions.

Almost anytime you look up at the sky, you can see clouds. **Clouds** are made up of little drops of water or ice. There are three main kinds of clouds.

Cirrus (SIR-es) clouds are thin and feathery. They are the highest clouds in the sky. They usually mean fair weather. But if they thicken, it could rain.

Cumulus (KUME-ya-les) clouds are puffy and cottony. Their shapes are always changing. You will see them low in the sky. They mean good weather. But piles of cumulus clouds make up **nimbus** clouds. These are black storm clouds. They are sometimes called thunderheads.

Stratus clouds are low in the sky, too. They look like wide, gray blankets. Drizzle and snow flurries fall from them.

1. What are clouds made of? little drops of water or ice
2. List three main kinds of clouds.
   1) cirrus
   2) stratus
   3) cumulus

35

Name: ____________

Reading Comprehension

Directions: Look at the pictures of clouds. Complete each sentence with the name of the cloud described. Use page 35 to help you.

cirrus	nimbus	cumulus	stratus

1. I am a low, flat, gray cloud. I bring drizzles or snow flurries. I am a ____ cloud. stratus

2. I am a black storm cloud. I am made up of many cumulus clouds. I have a flat top. I am a ____ cloud. nimbus
3. I am a thin, feathery cloud high in the sky. I usually mean good weather. I am a ____ cloud. cirrus

4. I am a puffy, cottony cloud. I won't ruin your picnic, because I mean fair weather. I am a ____ cloud. cumulus

36

Name: ____________

Reading Comprehension

Directions: Read the story. Then answer the questions.

The giant panda lives in bamboo forests in the mountains of China. This is lucky, because bamboo is the panda's favorite food! Bamboo is a kind of woody grass. It grows to be very tall. Bamboo grows in tough shoots called stalks.

A panda may eat hundreds of stalks of bamboo in a day. One reason is that one stalk of bamboo isn't very filling! Another reason is that only the top on the stalk is tender enough to eat. Of course, pandas think bamboo is delicious!

1. Where do giant pandas live? in the mountains of China
2. What is a panda's favorite food? bamboo
3. What is bamboo? a kind of woody grass
4. Write two reasons why pandas eat so many stalks of bamboo everyday.
   1) bamboo isn't very filling
   2) only the top of the stalk is tender enough to eat.

37

Name: ________

Reading Comprehension

Directions: Read the story. Then answer the questions.

In 1972, the Chinese people gave two giant pandas to the American people. The pandas lived at the National Zoo in Washington, D.C. for many years. At the time, they were the only giant pandas living in America.

The girl panda's name was Ling-Ling. That means "cute little girl" in Chinese. She died in 1992. The boy panda's name is Hsing-Hsing (shing-shing). It means "new."

1. How many giant pandas lived in America?
two
2. Where did these pandas live?
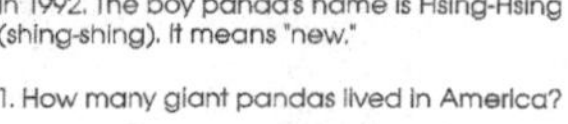
at the National Zoo in Washington, D.C.
3. What were the names of the giant pandas that came to America?

Ling-Ling and Hsing-Hsing
4. What do their names mean?
"cute little girl" (Ling-Ling)
"new" (Hsing-Hsing)

38

Name: ________

Reading Comprehension

Directions: Read the story. Then answer the questions.

Have you ever seen a tree that has been cut down? If so, you may have seen many circles in the trunk. These are called the **annual rings**. You can tell how old a tree is by counting these rings.

Trees have these rings because they grow a new layer of wood every year. The new layer grows right below the bark. In a year when there is a lot of rain and sunlight, the tree grows faster; the annual ring that year will be thick. When there is not much rain or sunlight, the tree grows slower and the ring is thin.

Circle the correct answer.

1. The annual ring of a tree tells how big the tree is. True (False)
2. Each year, a new layer of wood grows on top of the bark. True (False)
3. In a year with lots of rain and sunlight, the annual ring will be thick. (True) False
4. Trees grow faster when there is more rain and sunlight. (True) False
5. How old was the tree on this page? 16 years old

41

Name: ________

Reading Comprehension

Directions: Read the story. Then answer the questions.

Each year, as the hours of daylight grow shorter and colder weather comes, many types of trees lose their leaves. The falling of the leaves is so regular and amazing that the entire autumn season is called "fall."

The trees that lose their leaves are known as **deciduous** (dee-SID-you-us) trees. The word means "falling down." The leaves on these trees are wide, not like the needle-shaped leaves on pine and other **evergreen** trees. Trees lose water through their leaves, and wide leaves lose more water than the ones that look like needles. Water is very important to a tree. Because there is less water in the winter, the tree must drop its leaves to stay alive.

1. In what season do deciduous trees lose their leaves? fall
2. What are the trees called that do not lose their leaves?

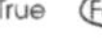
evergreen

Circle the correct answer.

3. Deciduous trees have needle-shaped leaves. True (False)
4. Trees drop their leaves to save water. (True) False

39

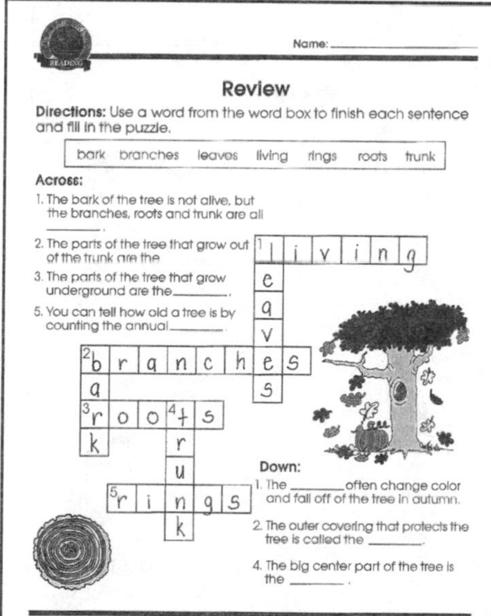

Name: ________

Review

Directions: Use a word from the word box to finish each sentence and fill in the puzzle.

bark branches leaves living rings roots trunk

Across:

1. The bark of the tree is not alive, but the branches, roots and trunk are all ________.
2. The parts of the tree that grow out of the trunk are the ________.
3. The parts of the tree that grow underground are the ________.
5. You can tell how old a tree is by counting the annual ________.

Down:

1. The ________ often change color and fall off of the tree in autumn.
2. The outer covering that protects the tree is called the ________.
4. The big center part of the tree is the ________.

42

Name: ________

Reading Comprehension

Directions: Read the story. Then answer the questions.

A tree has many living parts: roots, trunk, branches and leaves. The roots, trunk and branches grow each year. And every year new leaves grow on the branches. But there is a part of the tree that is not living. That part is the outer covering called the bark.

Bark is very hard and tough. It helps to protect the tree from harm. The bark stretches as the tree grows. On some trees, the bark stretches easily and looks smooth. On other trees, it doesn't stretch very easily. As these trees grow, the bark cracks and looks rough and bumpy.

1. What is the outer covering of the tree called? bark

Circle the correct answer.

2. If the bark of the tree stretches easily, the bark looks bumpy. True (False)
3. The bark helps to protect the tree from harm. Can you think of ways that a tree could be harmed?

Answers will vary.

40

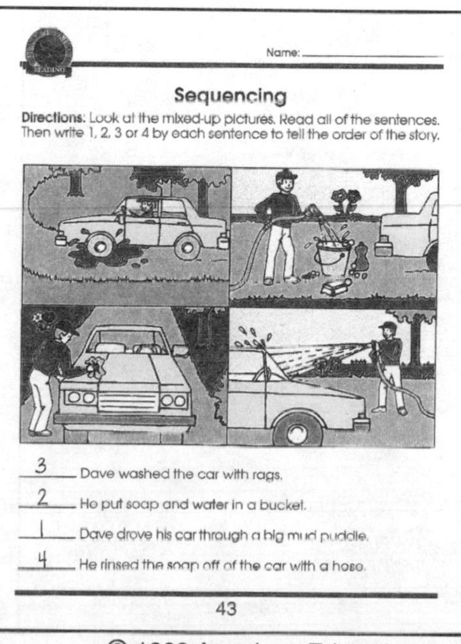

Name: ________

Sequencing

Directions: Look at the mixed-up pictures. Read all of the sentences. Then write 1, 2, 3 or 4 by each sentence to tell the order of the story.

3 Dave washed the car with rags.
2 He put soap and water in a bucket.
1 Dave drove his car through a big mud puddle.
4 He rinsed the soap off of the car with a hose.

43

Name: ____________

Sequencing

Directions: Fill in the blank spaces with what comes next in the series. The first one is done for you.

year	Wednesday	day	sixth	large
twenty	February	night	seventeen	mile
paragraph	winter	ocean		

1. Sunday, Monday, Tuesday, Wednesday
2. third, fourth, fifth, sixth
3. November, December, January, February
4. tiny, small, medium, large
5. fourteen, fifteen, sixteen, seventeen
6. morning, afternoon, evening, night
7. inch, foot, yard, mile
8. day, week, month, year
9. spring, summer, autumn, winter
10. five, ten, fifteen, twenty
11. letter, word, sentence, paragraph
12. second, minute, hour, day
13. stream, lake, river, ocean

44

Name: ____________

Sequencing

Directions: Read each story. Circle the phrase that tells what happened before.

1. Beth is very happy now that she has someone to play with. She hopes that her new sister will grow up quickly!

A few days ago . . .
Beth was sick.
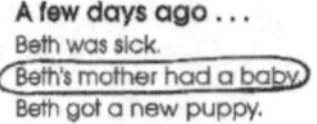
Beth's mother had a baby.
Beth got a new puppy.

2. Sara tried to mend the tear. She used a needle and thread to sew up the hole.

While playing, Sara had . . .
broken her bicycle.
lost her watch.
torn her shirt.

3. The movers took John's bike off the truck and put it in the garage. Next, they moved his bed into his new bedroom.

John's family . . .
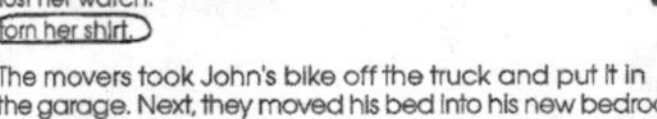
bought a new house.
went on vacation.
bought a new truck.

4. Katie picked out a book about dinosaurs. Jim, who likes sports, chose two books about baseball.

Katie and Jim . . .
went to the library.
went to the playground.
went to the grocery.

45

Name: ____________

Sequencing

Directions: Read each story. Circle the sentence that tells what might happen next.

1. Sam and Judy picked up their books and left the house. They walked to the bus stop. They got on a big yellow bus.

What will Sam and Judy do next?
They will go to school.
They will visit their grandmother.
They will go to the store.

2. Maggie and Matt were playing in the snow. They made a snowman with a black hat and a red scarf. Then the sun came out.

What might happen next?
It will snow again.
They will play in the sandbox.
The snowman will melt.

3. Megan put on a big floppy hat and funny clothes. She put green make-up on her face.

What will Megan do next?
She will go to school.

She will go to a costume party.
She will go to bed.

4. Mike was eating a hot dog. Suddenly he smelled smoke. He turned and saw a fire on the stove.

What will Mike do next?
He will watch the fire.
He will call for help.
He will finish his hot dog.

46

Name: ____________

Sequencing

Directions: Number these sentences from 1 to 6 to show the correct order of the story.

It is almost Valentine's Day . . .
3 She cut the paper into heart shapes and decorated them.
5 She put names and addresses on the envelopes.
1 Sally wanted to make valentines for her friends.
2 She got out paper, glue and scissors.
6 She put the valentines in the mailbox.
4 She bought envelopes to put them in.

The astronauts are going to the moon!
5 The spaceship takes the astronauts to the moon.
1 The astronauts must get into their space suits.
3 Then the countdown to take-off starts.
2 They climb into the spaceship.
4 Rockets blast the spaceship into space.
6 The astronauts walk on the moon.

47

Name: ____________

Sequencing

Directions: Number these sentences from 1 to 5 to show the correct order of the story.

Building a Treehouse
4 They had a beautiful treehouse!
2 They got wood and nails.
1 Jay and Lisa planned to build a treehouse.
5 Now, they like to eat lunch in their treehouse.
3 Lisa and Jay worked in the backyard for three days building the treehouse.

A School Play
5 Everyone clapped when the curtain closed.
4 The girl who played Snow White came onto the stage.
2 All the other school children went to the gym to see the play.
3 The stage curtain opened.
1 The third grade was going to put on a play about Snow White.

48

Name: ____________

Sequencing

Directions: Number these sentences from 1 to 8 to show the correct order of the story.

4 Jack's father called the family doctor.

8 Jack felt much better as his parents drove him home.

1 Jack woke up in the middle of the night with a terrible pain in his stomach.

5 The doctor told Jack's father to take Jack to the hospital.

2 Jack called his parents to come help him.

7 At the hospital, the doctors examined Jack. They said the problem was not serious. They told Jack's parents that he could go home.

3 Jack's mother took his temperature. He had a fever of 103 degrees.

6 On the way to the hospital, Jack rested in the backseat. He was worried.

49

Name: ____________

Review

Directions: Read the story. Then follow the directions.

The Magnifying Glass

Timmy's grandfather was reading the newspaper. He held something in his hand as he read. "What's that, Grandpa?" asked Timmy.

"It's a magnifying glass to help me see the words better," said Grandpa. He showed Timmy how holding the glass over a word made the word look bigger.

Timmy looked at a fly under the magnifying glass. The fly looked big! Timmy could even see the eye of the fly. "It's like magic!" he said.

Timmy wanted to explore the yard with Grandpa's magic glass. "Let's go to the store and buy one for you," said Grandpa. "Then I can finish reading my newspaper!"

Directions: Number these sentences from 1 to 5 to show the correct order of the story.

3 Timmy looked at a fly under the magnifying glass.

1 Timmy's grandfather was reading.

2 Grandpa showed Timmy how the magnifying glass worked.

4 Timmy wanted to take the magnifying glass outside.

5 Grandpa is going to buy Timmy a magnifying glass.

50

Name: ____________

Noting Details

Directions: Read the story. Then answer the questions.

Thomas Edison was one of America's greatest inventors. An **inventor** thinks up new machines and new ways of doing things. Edison was born in Milan, Ohio in 1847. He went to school for only three months. His teacher thought he was not very smart because he asked so many questions.

Edison liked to experiment. He had many wonderful ideas. He invented the light bulb and the phonograph (record player).

Thomas Edison died in 1931, but we still use many of his inventions today.

1. What is an inventor?
A person who thinks up new machines and new ways of doing things
2. Where was Thomas Edison born?
Milan, Ohio
3. How long did he go to school?
three months
4. What are two of Edison's inventions?
the light bulb and the phonograph

51

Name: ____________

Noting Details

Directions: Read the story. Then answer the questions.

The giant panda is much smaller than a brown bear or a polar bear. In fact, a horse weighs about four times as much as a giant panda. So why is it called "giant"? It is giant next to another kind of panda called the red panda.

The red panda also lives in China. The red panda is about the size of a fox. It has a long, fluffy, striped tail and beautiful reddish fur. It looks very much like a raccoon.

Many people think the giant pandas are bears. They look like bears. Even the word panda is Chinese for "white bear." But because of its relationship to the red panda, many scientists now believe that the panda is really more like a raccoon!

1. Why is the giant panda called "giant"?
It is larger than the red panda.
2. Where does the red panda live?
in China
3. How big is the red panda?
about the size of a fox
4. What animal does the red panda look like?
a raccoon
5. What does the word panda mean?
"white bear"

52

Name: ____________

Noting Details

Directions: Read the story. Then answer the questions.

Giant pandas do not live in families like people do. The only pandas that live together are mothers and their babies. Newborn pandas are very tiny and helpless. They weigh only five ounces when they are born—about the weight of a stick of butter! They are born with their eyes closed, and they have no teeth.

It takes about three years for a panda to grow up. When full grown, a giant panda weighs about 300 pounds and is five to six feet tall. Once a panda is grown up, it leaves its mother and goes off to live by itself.

1. What pandas live together? mothers and their babies
2. How much do pandas weigh when they are born? about five ounces
3. Why do newborn pandas live with their mothers? They are very tiny and helpless.
4. When is a panda full grown? at three years old
5. How big is a grown-up panda? five to six feet tall and 300 pounds.

53

Name: ____________

Following Directions

Directions: Learning to follow directions is very important. Use the map to find your way to different houses.

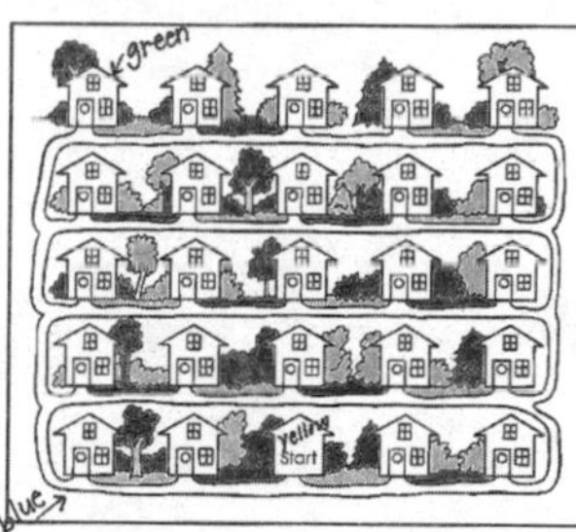

1. Color the start house yellow.
2. Go north 2 houses, and east two houses.
3. Go north 2 houses, and west 4 houses.
4. Color the house green.
5. Start at the yellow house.
6. Go east 1 house, and north 3 houses.
7. Go west 3 houses, and south 3 houses.
8. Color the house blue.

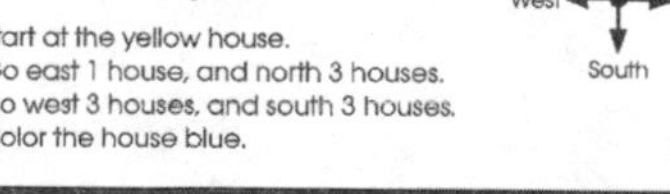

54

Name: ____________

Following Directions

Origami is the Japanese art of paper folding. No scissors or glue are needed.

Directions: Use a piece of plain paper. Follow the steps listed below.

1. Fold the paper in half the long way, crease and unfold.
2. Fold the sides up to the middle crease. Keep folded.
3. Fold the corners down to the middle.

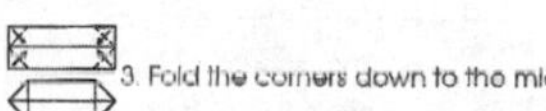

4. Fold the corners down to the middle again.

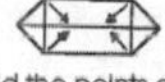 

5. Fold the points down to the middle.

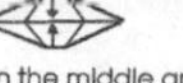 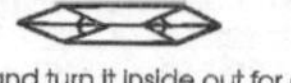

6. Open the middle and turn it inside out for a boat, or flip it over and wear it as a hat!

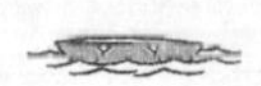 

What else can you make using origami? Answers will vary.

55

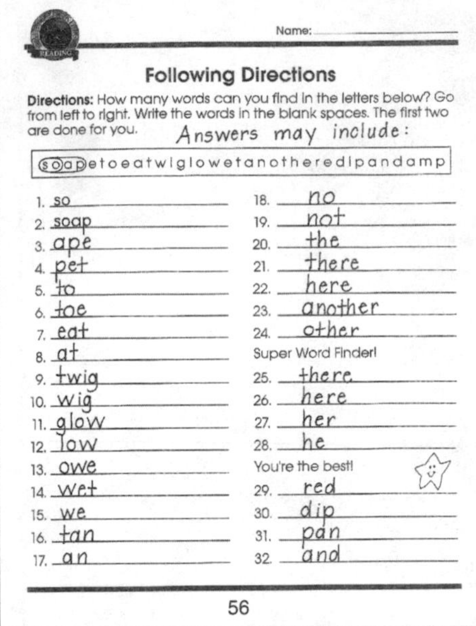

Name: ____________

Following Directions

Directions: How many words can you find in the letters below? Go from left to right. Write the words in the blank spaces. The first two are done for you.

Answers may include:

soapetoeatwiglowetanotheredipandamp

1. so		18. no	
2. soap		19. not	
3. ape		20. the	
4. pet		21. there	
5. to		22. here	
6. toe		23. another	
7. eat		24. other	
8. at		Super Word Finder!	
9. twig		25. there	
10. wig		26. here	
11. glow		27. her	
12. low		28. he	
13. owe		You're the best!	
14. wet		29. red	
15. we		30. dip	
16. tan		31. pan	
17. an		32. and	

56

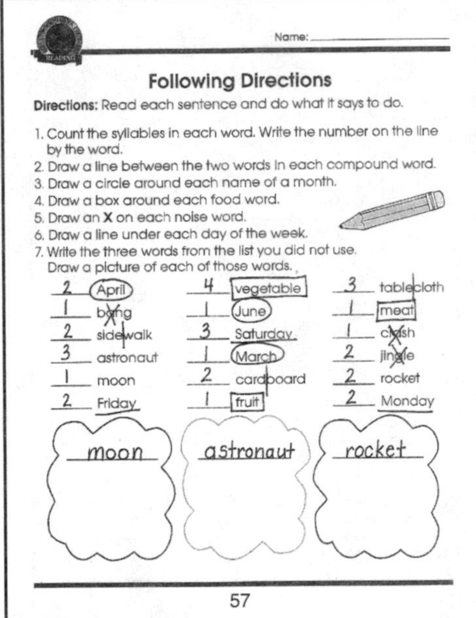

Name: ____________

Following Directions

Directions: Read each sentence and do what it says to do.

1. Count the syllables in each word. Write the number on the line by the word.
2. Draw a line between the two words in each compound word.
3. Draw a circle around each name of a month.
4. Draw a box around each food word.
5. Draw an **X** on each noise word.
6. Draw a line under each day of the week.
7. Write the three words from the list you did not use. Draw a picture of each of those words.

2 April	4 vegetable	3 tablecloth
1 bang	1 June	1 meat
2 sidewalk	3 Saturday	1 crash
3 astronaut	1 March	2 jingle
1 moon	2 cardboard	2 rocket
2 Friday	1 fruit	2 Monday

moon — astronaut — rocket

57

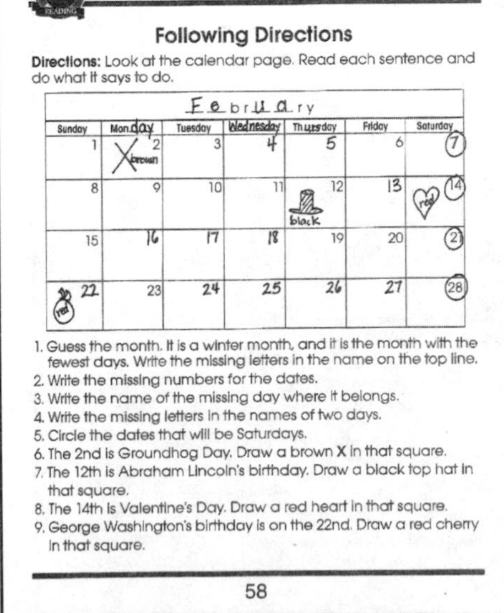

Name: ____________

Following Directions

Directions: Look at the calendar page. Read each sentence and do what it says to do.

February

Sunday	Monday	Tuesday	Wednesday	Thursday	Friday	Saturday
	1	2 (brown X)	3	4	5	6	7
8	9	10	11	12 (black hat)	13	14 (red heart)
15	16	17	18	19	20	21
22 (red cherry)	23	24	25	26	27	28

1. Guess the month. It is a winter month, and it is the month with the fewest days. Write the missing letters in the name on the top line.
2. Write the missing numbers for the dates.
3. Write the name of the missing day where it belongs.
4. Write the missing letters in the names of two days.
5. Circle the dates that will be Saturdays.
6. The 2nd is Groundhog Day. Draw a brown **X** in that square.
7. The 12th is Abraham Lincoln's birthday. Draw a black top hat in that square.
8. The 14th is Valentine's Day. Draw a red heart in that square.
9. George Washington's birthday is on the 22nd. Draw a red cherry in that square.

58

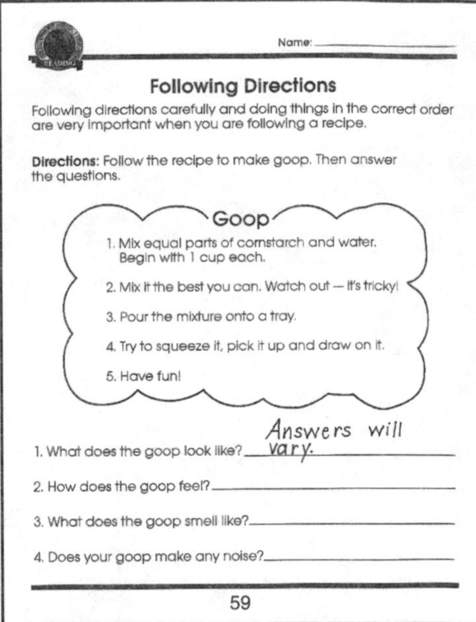

Name: ____________

Following Directions

Following directions carefully and doing things in the correct order are very important when you are following a recipe.

Directions: Follow the recipe to make goop. Then answer the questions.

Goop

1. Mix equal parts of cornstarch and water. Begin with 1 cup each.
2. Mix it the best you can. Watch out — it's tricky!
3. Pour the mixture onto a tray.
4. Try to squeeze it, pick it up and draw on it.
5. Have fun!

1. What does the goop look like? Answers will vary.
2. How does the goop feel? ____________
3. What does the goop smell like? ____________
4. Does your goop make any noise? ____________

59

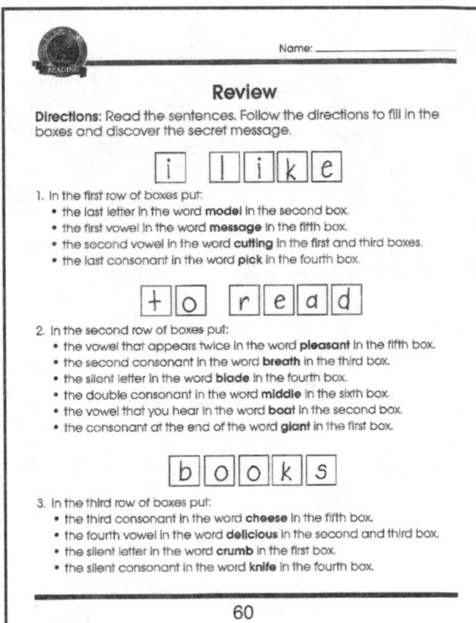

Name: ____________

Review

Directions: Read the sentences. Follow the directions to fill in the boxes and discover the secret message.

i like

1. In the first row of boxes put:
   - the last letter in the word **model** in the second box.
   - the first vowel in the word **message** in the fifth box.
   - the second vowel in the word **cutting** in the first and third boxes.
   - the last consonant in the word **pick** in the fourth box.

to read

2. In the second row of boxes put:
   - the vowel that appears twice in the word **pleasant** in the fifth box.
   - the second consonant in the word **breath** in the third box.
   - the silent letter in the word **blade** in the fourth box.
   - the double consonant in the word **middle** in the sixth box.
   - the vowel that you hear in the word **boat** in the second box.
   - the consonant at the end of the word **giant** in the first box.

books

3. In the third row of boxes put:
   - the third consonant in the word **cheese** in the fifth box.
   - the fourth vowel in the word **delicious** in the second and third box.
   - the silent letter in the word **crumb** in the first box.
   - the silent consonant in the word **knife** in the fourth box.

60

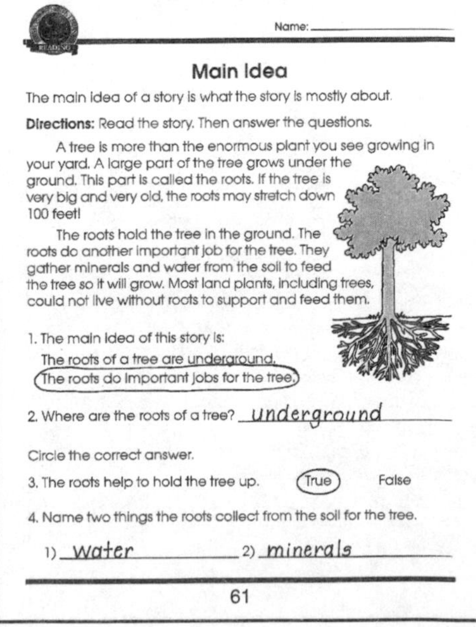

Name: ____________

Main Idea

The main idea of a story is what the story is mostly about.

Directions: Read the story. Then answer the questions.

A tree is more than the enormous plant you see growing in your yard. A large part of the tree grows under the ground. This part is called the roots. If the tree is very big and very old, the roots may stretch down 100 feet!

The roots hold the tree in the ground. The roots do another important job for the tree. They gather minerals and water from the soil to feed the tree so it will grow. Most land plants, including trees, could not live without roots to support and feed them.

1. The main idea of this story is:
   The roots of a tree are underground.
   (The roots do important jobs for the tree.)
2. Where are the roots of a tree? underground

Circle the correct answer.

3. The roots help to hold the tree up. (True) False
4. Name two things the roots collect from the soil for the tree.
   1) water 2) minerals

61

Name: ______________

Main Idea

Directions: Read about spiders. Then answer the questions.

Many people think spiders are insects, but they are not. Spiders are the same size as insects, and they look like insects in some ways. But there are three ways to tell a spider from an insect. Insects have six legs, and spiders have eight legs. Insects have antennae, but spiders do not. An insect's body is divided into three parts; a spider's body is divided into only two parts.

1. The main idea of this story is:

Spiders are like insects.

(Spiders are like insects in some ways, but they are not insects.)

2. What are three ways to tell a spider from an insect?

1) spiders have eight legs; insects have six.

2) insects have antennae; spiders do not.

3) insects have three body parts; spiders have two

Circle the correct answer.

3. Spiders are the same size as insects. (True) False

62

Name: ______________

Main Idea

Directions: Read about the giant panda. Then answer the questions.

Giant pandas are among the world's favorite animals. They look like big, cuddly stuffed toys. There are not very many pandas left in the world. You may have to travel a long way to see one.

The only place on Earth where pandas live in the wild is in the bamboo forests of the mountains of China. It is hard to see pandas in the forest because they are very shy. They hide among the many bamboo trees. It also is hard to see pandas because there are so few of them. Scientists think there may be less than 1,000 pandas living in the mountains of China.

1. Write a sentence that tells the main idea of this story:

There are very few pandas left in the world.

2. What are two reasons that it is hard to see pandas in the wild?

1) They hide among the bamboo trees.

2) There are very few pandas.

3. How many pandas are believed to be living in the mountains of China?

fewer than 1,000.

63

Name: ______________

Main Idea

Directions: Read the story. Then answer the questions.

Because bamboo is very important to pandas, they have special body features that help them eat it. The panda's front foot is like a hand. But, instead of four fingers and a thumb, the panda has five fingers and an extra-long wrist bone. With its special front foot, the panda can easily pick up the stalks of bamboo. It also can hold the bamboo more tightly than it could with a hand like ours.

Bamboo stalks are very tough. The panda uses its big heavy head, large jaws and big back teeth to chew. Pandas eat the bamboo first by peeling the outside of the stalk. They do this by moving their front feet from side to side while holding the stalk in their teeth. Then they bite off a piece of the bamboo and chew it with their strong jaws.

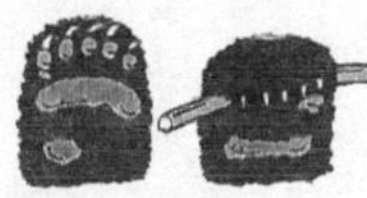

1. Write a sentence that tells the main idea of this story.

Pandas have special body features to help them eat bamboo.

2. Instead of four fingers and a thumb, the panda has

five fingers and an extra-long wrist bone.

3. Bamboo is very tender. True  (False)

64

Name: ______________

Review

Directions: Read the story. Then answer the questions.

Hsing-Hsing lives in a special Panda House in the National Zoo. He has a large air-conditioned cage (the temperature is kept at 50 degrees Fahrenheit) and a sleeping den. Hsing-Hsing can play in a big yard. The yard has bamboo trees growing in it.

It is very expensive to feed pandas. Besides bamboo, they also like rice, apples, bone meal, honey, carrots, cat food and dog biscuits, sweet potatoes, cantaloupes and grass. It costs about as much to feed two pandas as it does to feed three elephants!

1. Write a sentence that tells the main idea of this story.

Pandas need special food and cages.

2. At what temperature do you need to keep panda cages?

50 degrees Fahrenheit

3. Name three things other than bamboo that pandas like to eat.

Answers may include:

1) rice 3) honey

2) apples

4. How expensive is it to feed two pandas?

as much as it costs to feed three elephants

65

Name: ______________

Review

Directions: Read the story. Then answer the questions.

There are many different kinds of robots. One special kind of robot takes the place of people in guiding airplanes and ships. They are called "automatic pilots." These robots are really computers programmed to do just one special job. They have the information to control the speed and direction of the plane or ship.

Robots are used for many jobs in which a person can't get too close because of danger, such as in exploding a bomb. Robots can be controlled from a distance. This is called "remote control." These robots are very important in studying space. In the future, robots will be used to work on space stations and on other planets.

1. The main idea of this story is:

Robots are used for many different jobs.

2. Why are robots good in dangerous jobs?

They are machines. They can't be hurt the way people can.

3. What is "remote control"?

controlled from a distance

4. What will robots be used for in the future?

to work on space stations and on other planets

What would you have a robot do for you?

answers will vary.

66

Name: ______________

Inference

Inference is using logic to figure out what is not directly told.

Directions: Read the story. Then answer the questions.

Many thousands of people go to the National Zoo each year to see Hsing-Hsing. Sometimes, there are as many as 1,000 visitors in one hour! Like all pandas, Hsing-Hsing spends most of his time sleeping. But because pandas are so rare, most people think it is exciting to see even a sleeping panda!

1. Popular means well-liked. Do you think giant pandas are popular?

Yes.

2. What clue do you have that pandas are popular?

They have as many as 1,000 visitors an hour.

3. What do most visitors see Hsing-Hsing doing?

sleeping

67

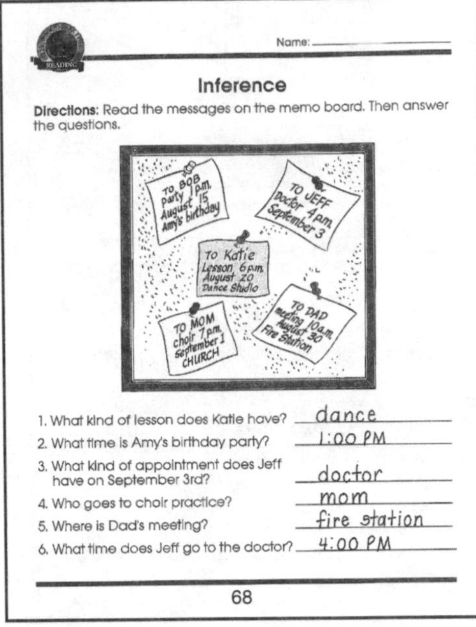

Name: ____________

Inference

Directions: Read the messages on the memo board. Then answer the questions.

1. What kind of lesson does Katie have? dance
2. What time is Amy's birthday party? 1:00 PM
3. What kind of appointment does Jeff have on September 3rd? doctor
4. Who goes to choir practice? mom
5. Where is Dad's meeting? fire station
6. What time does Jeff go to the doctor? 4:00 PM

68

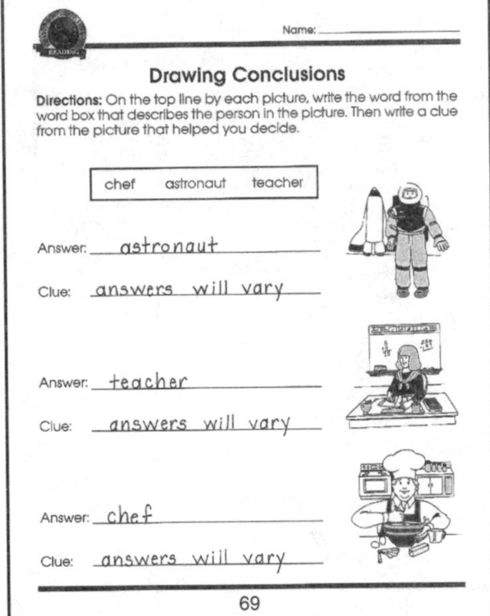

Name: ____________

Drawing Conclusions

Directions: On the top line by each picture, write the word from the word box that describes the person in the picture. Then write a clue from the picture that helped you decide.

chef	astronaut	teacher

Answer: astronaut

Clue: answers will vary

Answer: teacher

Clue: answers will vary

Answer: chef

Clue: answers will vary

69

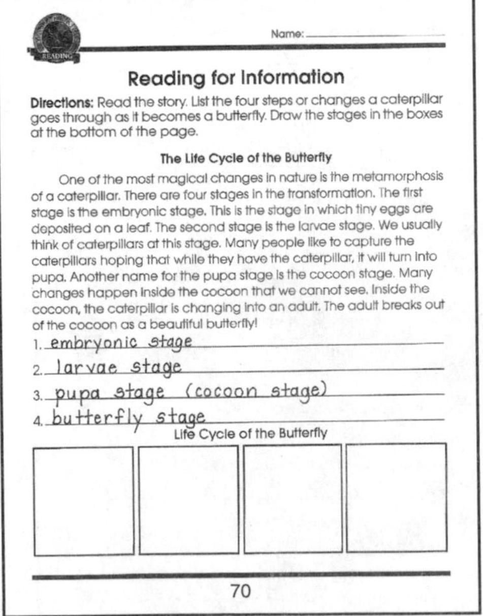

Name: ____________

Reading for Information

Directions: Read the story. List the four steps or changes a caterpillar goes through as it becomes a butterfly. Draw the stages in the boxes at the bottom of the page.

The Life Cycle of the Butterfly

One of the most magical changes in nature is the metamorphosis of a caterpillar. There are four stages in the transformation. The first stage is the embryonic stage. This is the stage in which tiny eggs are deposited on a leaf. The second stage is the larvae stage. We usually think of caterpillars at this stage. Many people like to capture the caterpillars hoping that while they have the caterpillar, it will turn into pupa. Another name for the pupa stage is the cocoon stage. Many changes happen inside the cocoon that we cannot see. Inside the cocoon, the caterpillar is changing into an adult. The adult breaks out of the cocoon as a beautiful butterfly!

1. embryonic stage
2. larvae stage
3. pupa stage (cocoon stage)
4. butterfly stage

Life Cycle of the Butterfly

70

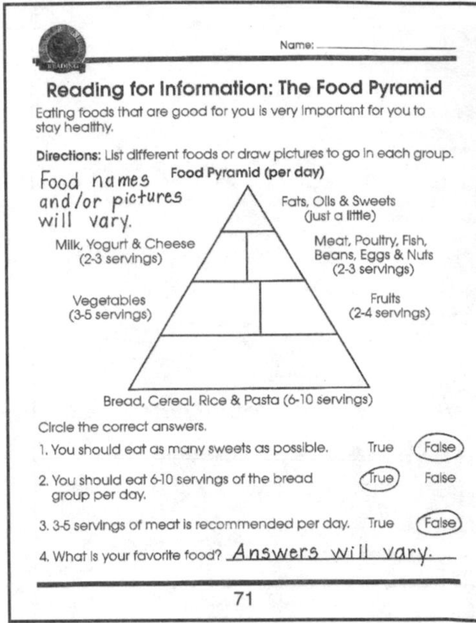

Name: ____________

Reading for Information: The Food Pyramid

Eating foods that are good for you is very important for you to stay healthy.

Directions: List different foods or draw pictures to go in each group.

Food names and/or pictures will vary.

Circle the correct answers.

1. You should eat as many sweets as possible. True (False)
2. You should eat 6-10 servings of the bread group per day. (True) False
3. 3-5 servings of meat is recommended per day. True (False)
4. What is your favorite food? Answers will vary.

71

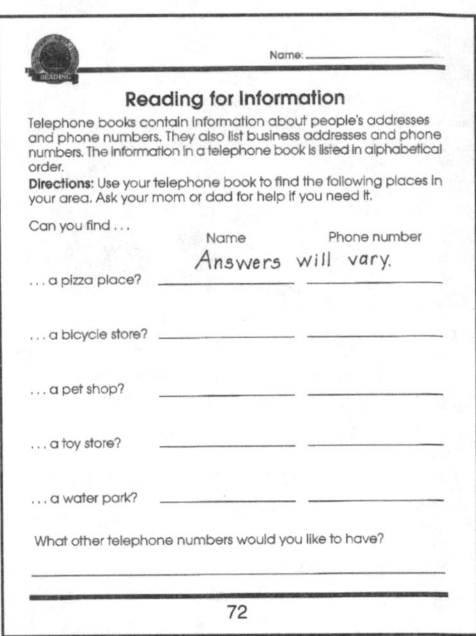

Name: ____________

Reading for Information

Telephone books contain information about people's addresses and phone numbers. They also list business addresses and phone numbers. The information in a telephone book is listed in alphabetical order.

Directions: Use your telephone book to find the following places in your area. Ask your mom or dad for help if you need it.

Can you find . . .

	Name	Phone number
. . . a pizza place?	Answers will vary.	
. . . a bicycle store?		
. . . a pet shop?		
. . . a toy store?		
. . . a water park?		

What other telephone numbers would you like to have?

72

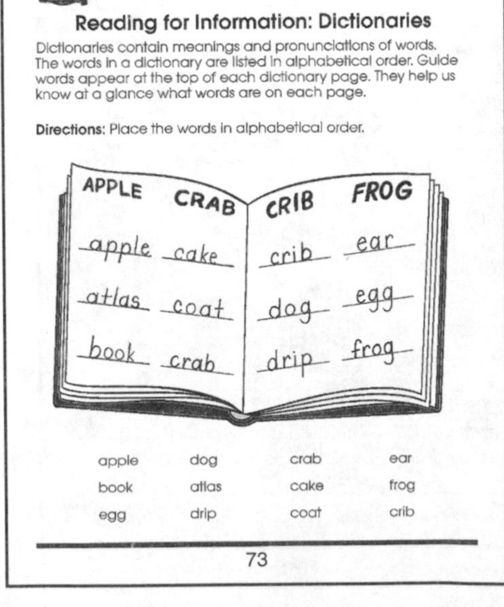

Name: ____________

Reading for Information: Dictionaries

Dictionaries contain meanings and pronunciations of words. The words in a dictionary are listed in alphabetical order. Guide words appear at the top of each dictionary page. They help us know at a glance what words are on each page.

Directions: Place the words in alphabetical order.

APPLE	CRAB	CRIB	FROG
apple	cake	crib	ear
atlas	coat	dog	egg
book	crab	drip	frog

apple	dog	crab	ear
book	atlas	cake	frog
egg	drip	coat	crib

73

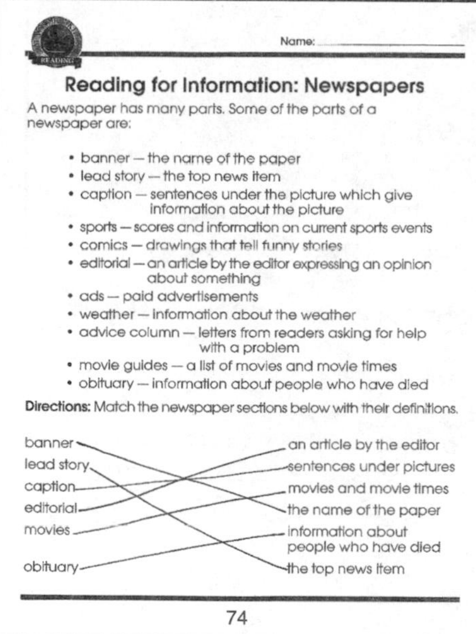

Name: ____________

Reading for Information: Newspapers

A newspaper has many parts. Some of the parts of a newspaper are:

- banner — the name of the paper
- lead story — the top news item
- caption — sentences under the picture which give information about the picture
- sports — scores and information on current sports events
- comics — drawings that tell funny stories
- editorial — an article by the editor expressing an opinion about something
- ads — paid advertisements
- weather — information about the weather
- advice column — letters from readers asking for help with a problem
- movie guides — a list of movies and movie times
- obituary — information about people who have died

Directions: Match the newspaper sections below with their definitions.

banner	an article by the editor
lead story	sentences under pictures
caption	movies and movie times
editorial	the name of the paper
movies	information about people who have died
obituary	the top news item

74

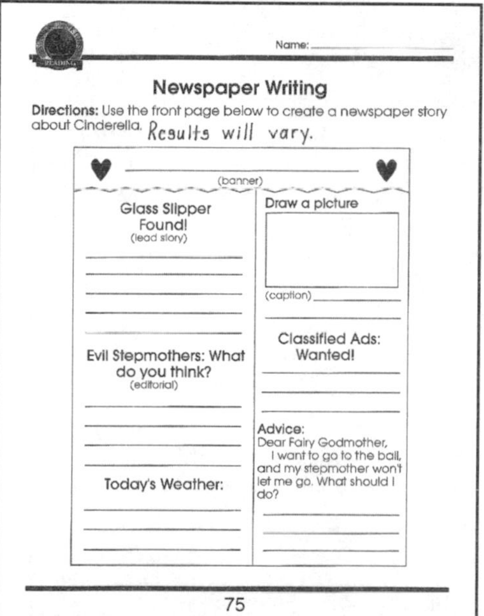

Name: ____________

Newspaper Writing

Directions: Use the front page below to create a newspaper story about Cinderella. Results will vary.

(banner)

Glass Slipper Found!
(lead story)

Draw a picture

(caption)

Evil Stepmothers: What do you think?
(editorial)

Classified Ads: Wanted!

Today's Weather:

Advice:
Dear Fairy Godmother,
I want to go to the ball, and my stepmother won't let me go. What should I do?

75

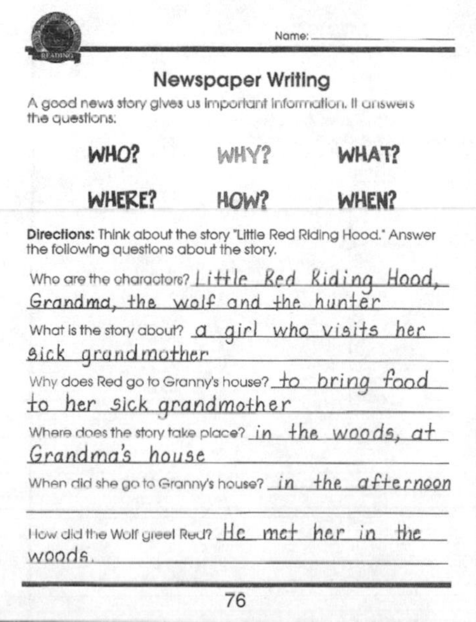

Name: ____________

Newspaper Writing

A good news story gives us important information. It answers the questions:

WHO? WHY? WHAT?

WHERE? HOW? WHEN?

Directions: Think about the story "Little Red Riding Hood." Answer the following questions about the story.

Who are the characters? Little Red Riding Hood, Grandma, the wolf and the hunter

What is the story about? a girl who visits her sick grandmother

Why does Red go to Granny's house? to bring food to her sick grandmother

Where does the story take place? in the woods, at Grandma's house

When did she go to Granny's house? in the afternoon

How did the Wolf greet Red? He met her in the woods.

76

Name: ____________

Fantasy and Reality

Something that is **real** could actually happen. Something that is **fantasy** is not real. It could not happen.

Examples: Real: Dogs can bark.
Fantasy: Dogs can fly.

Directions: Look at the sentences below. Write **real** or **fantasy** next to each sentence.

1. My cat can talk to me. fantasy
2. Witches ride brooms and cast spells. fantasy
3. Dad can mow the lawn. real
4. I ride a magic carpet to school. fantasy
5. I have a man-eating tree. fantasy
6. My sandbox has toys in it. real
7. Mom can bake chocolate chip cookies. real
8. Mark's garden has tomatoes and corn in it. real
9. Jack grows candy and ice cream in his garden. fantasy
10. I make my bed everyday. real

Write your own **real** sentence. Answers will vary.

Write your own **fantasy** sentence. Answers will vary.

77

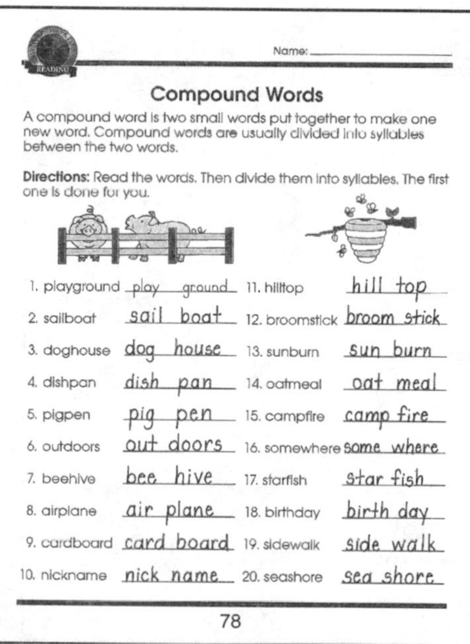

Name: ____________

Compound Words

A compound word is two small words put together to make one new word. Compound words are usually divided into syllables between the two words.

Directions: Read the words. Then divide them into syllables. The first one is done for you.

1. playground	play ground	11. hilltop	hill top
2. sailboat	sail boat	12. broomstick	broom stick
3. doghouse	dog house	13. sunburn	sun burn
4. dishpan	dish pan	14. oatmeal	oat meal
5. pigpen	pig pen	15. campfire	camp fire
6. outdoors	out doors	16. somewhere	some where
7. beehive	bee hive	17. starfish	star fish
8. airplane	air plane	18. birthday	birth day
9. cardboard	card board	19. sidewalk	side walk
10. nickname	nick name	20. seashore	sea shore

78

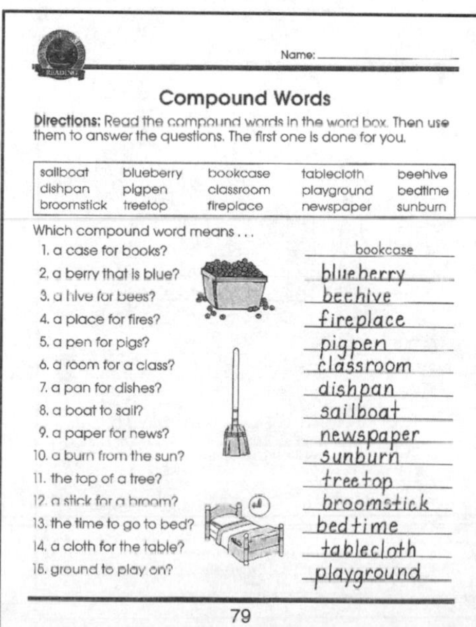

Name: ____________

Compound Words

Directions: Read the compound words in the word box. Then use them to answer the questions. The first one is done for you.

sailboat	blueberry	bookcase	tablecloth	beehive
dishpan	pigpen	classroom	playground	bedtime
broomstick	treetop	fireplace	newspaper	sunburn

Which compound word means . . .

1. a case for books? bookcase
2. a berry that is blue? blueberry
3. a hive for bees? beehive
4. a place for fires? fireplace
5. a pen for pigs? pigpen
6. a room for a class? classroom
7. a pan for dishes? dishpan
8. a boat to sail? sailboat
9. a paper for news? newspaper
10. a burn from the sun? sunburn
11. the top of a tree? treetop
12. a stick for a broom? broomstick
13. the time to go to bed? bedtime
14. a cloth for the table? tablecloth
15. ground to play on? playground

79

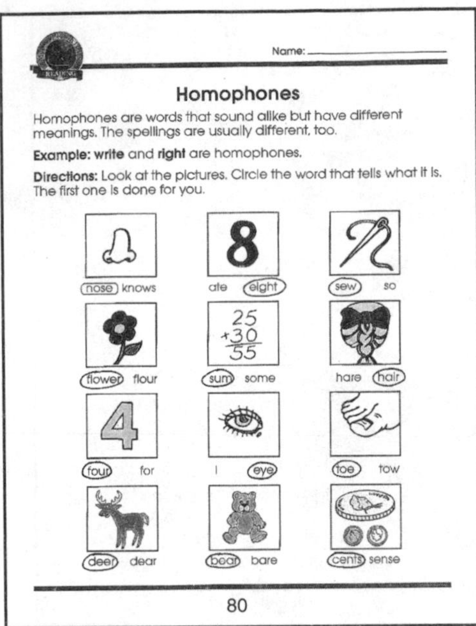

Name: ___

Homophones

Homophones are words that sound alike but have different meanings. The spellings are usually different, too.

Example: write and **right** are homophones.

Directions: Look at the pictures. Circle the word that tells what it is. The first one is done for you.

(nose) knows	ate (eight)	(sew) so
(flower) flour	(sum) some	hare (hair)
(four) for	I (eye)	(toe) tow
(deer) dear	(bear) bare	(cents) sense

80

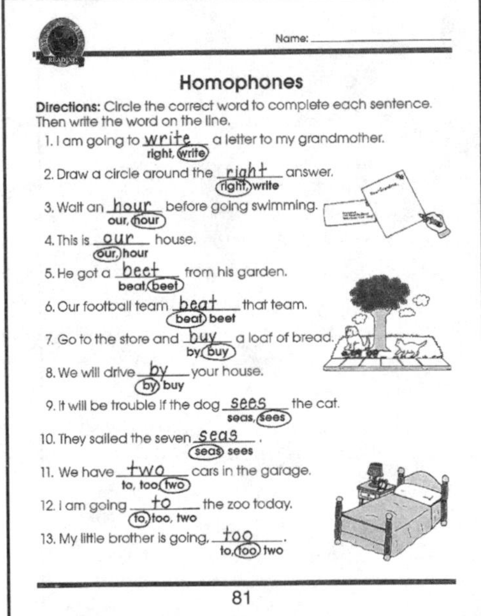

Name: ___

Homophones

Directions: Circle the correct word to complete each sentence. Then write the word on the line.

1. I am going to write a letter to my grandmother. (right, (write))
2. Draw a circle around the right answer. ((right), write)
3. Wait an hour before going swimming. (our, (hour))
4. This is our house. ((our), hour)
5. He got a beet from his garden. (beat, (beet))
6. Our football team beat that team. ((beat), beet)
7. Go to the store and buy a loaf of bread. (by, (buy))
8. We will drive by your house. ((by), buy)
9. It will be trouble if the dog sees the cat. (seas, (sees))
10. They sailed the seven seas. ((seas), sees)
11. We have two cars in the garage. (to, too, (two))
12. I am going to the zoo today. ((to), too, two)
13. My little brother is going, too. (to, (too), two)

81

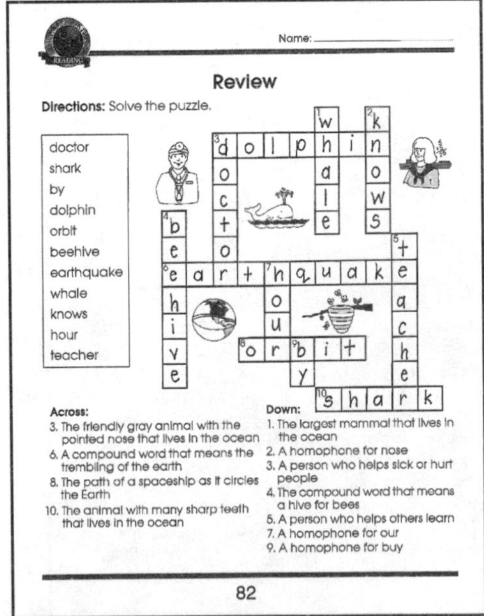

Name: ___

Review

Directions: Solve the puzzle.

doctor
shark
by
dolphin
orbit
beehive
earthquake
whale
knows
hour
teacher

Across:

3. The friendly gray animal with the pointed nose that lives in the ocean
6. A compound word that means the trembling of the earth
8. The path of a spaceship as it circles the Earth
10. The animal with many sharp teeth that lives in the ocean

Down:

1. The largest mammal that lives in the ocean
2. A homophone for nose
3. A person who helps sick or hurt people
4. The compound word that means a hive for bees
5. A person who helps others learn
7. A homophone for our
9. A homophone for buy

82

Name: ___

Homophone Match

Directions: Cut out the homophones cards on this page and the next page. Mix them up and lay them facedown. Turn over two cards at a time and try to find the matching homophones. When you get a pair, you keep them! The person with the most pairs, wins.

too	two	know	no
some	sum	shown	shone
threw	through	new	knew
pair	pear	there	their
eight	ate	fair	fare

83

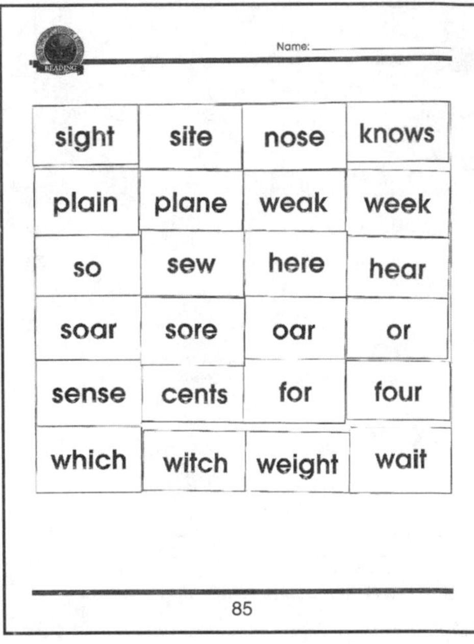

Name: ___

sight	site	nose	knows
plain	plane	weak	week
so	sew	here	hear
soar	sore	oar	or
sense	cents	for	four
which	witch	weight	wait

85

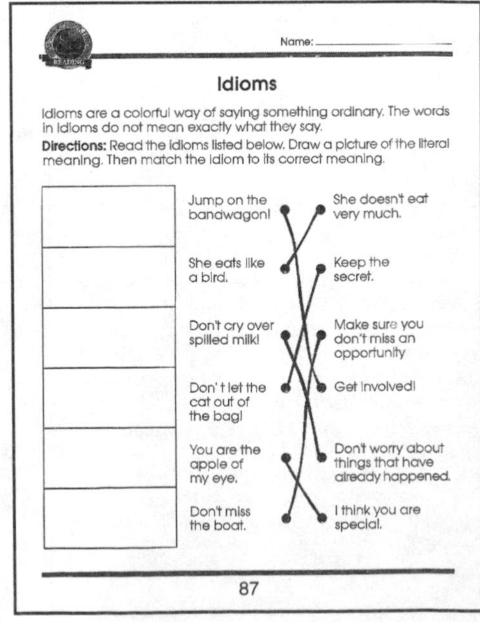

Name: ___

Idioms

Idioms are a colorful way of saying something ordinary. The words in idioms do not mean exactly what they say.

Directions: Read the idioms listed below. Draw a picture of the literal meaning. Then match the idiom to its correct meaning.

Jump on the bandwagon!	She doesn't eat very much.
She eats like a bird.	Keep the secret.
Don't cry over spilled milk!	Make sure you don't miss an opportunity
Don't let the cat out of the bag!	Get involved!
You are the apple of my eye.	Don't worry about things that have already happened.
Don't miss the boat.	I think you are special.

87

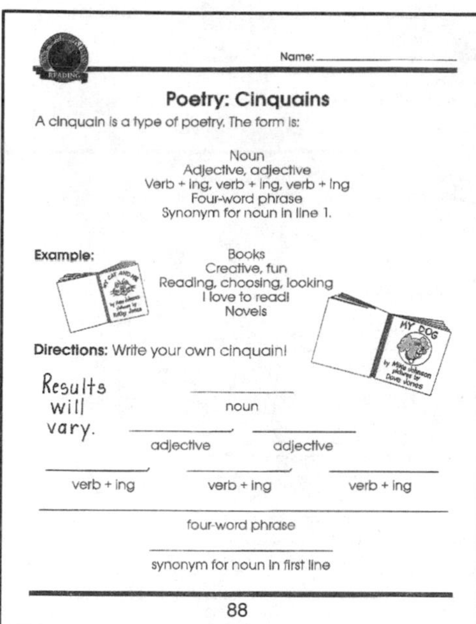

Name: ____________

Poetry: Cinquains

A cinquain is a type of poetry. The form is:

Noun
Adjective, adjective
Verb + ing, verb + ing, verb + ing
Four-word phrase
Synonym for noun in line 1.

Example:

Books
Creative, fun
Reading, choosing, looking
I love to read!
Novels

Directions: Write your own cinquain!

Results will vary.

______ noun

______ adjective ______ adjective

______ verb + ing ______ verb + ing ______ verb + ing

______ four-word phrase

______ synonym for noun in first line

88

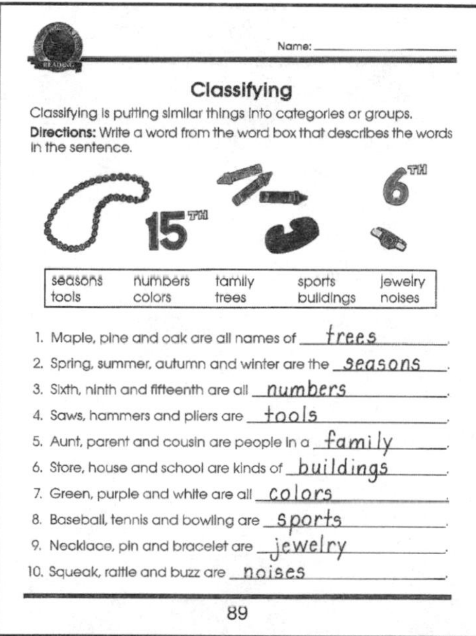

Name: ____________

Classifying

Classifying is putting similar things into categories or groups.

Directions: Write a word from the word box that describes the words in the sentence.

seasons	numbers	family	sports	jewelry
tools	colors	trees	buildings	noises

1. Maple, pine and oak are all names of trees.
2. Spring, summer, autumn and winter are the seasons.
3. Sixth, ninth and fifteenth are all numbers.
4. Saws, hammers and pliers are tools.
5. Aunt, parent and cousin are people in a family.
6. Store, house and school are kinds of buildings.
7. Green, purple and white are all colors.
8. Baseball, tennis and bowling are sports.
9. Necklace, pin and bracelet are jewelry.
10. Squeak, rattle and buzz are noises.

89

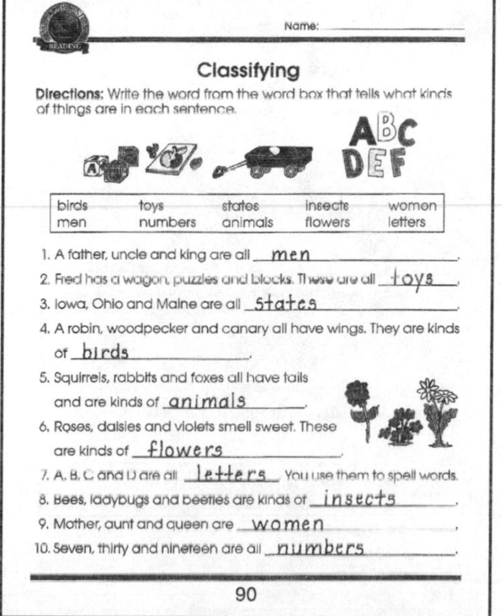

Name: ____________

Classifying

Directions: Write the word from the word box that tells what kinds of things are in each sentence.

birds	toys	states	insects	women
men	numbers	animals	flowers	letters

1. A father, uncle and king are all men.
2. Fred has a wagon, puzzles and blocks. These are all toys.
3. Iowa, Ohio and Maine are all states.
4. A robin, woodpecker and canary all have wings. They are kinds of birds.
5. Squirrels, rabbits and foxes all have tails and are kinds of animals.
6. Roses, daisies and violets smell sweet. These are kinds of flowers.
7. A, B, C and D are all letters. You use them to spell words.
8. Bees, ladybugs and beetles are kinds of insects.
9. Mother, aunt and queen are women.
10. Seven, thirty and nineteen are all numbers.

90

Name: ____________

Classifying

Directions: After each sentence, write three words from the word box that belong.

eagle	whistle	horn	frog
dime	wheel	throat	ball
sun	airplane	penny	marble
banana	balloon	dollar	heart
camel	grasshopper	horse	kangaroo
chipmunk	lemon	butterfly	mouth

1. These are things that can hop.
grasshopper frog kangaroo
2. These things all have wings.
eagle butterfly airplane
3. These are types of money.
dime penny dollar
4. These are four-legged animals.
camel chipmunk horse
5. These are parts of your body.
throat mouth heart
6. These things are yellow.
sun banana lemon
7. These things can roll.
wheel marble ball
8. These are things you can blow.
whistle balloon horn

91

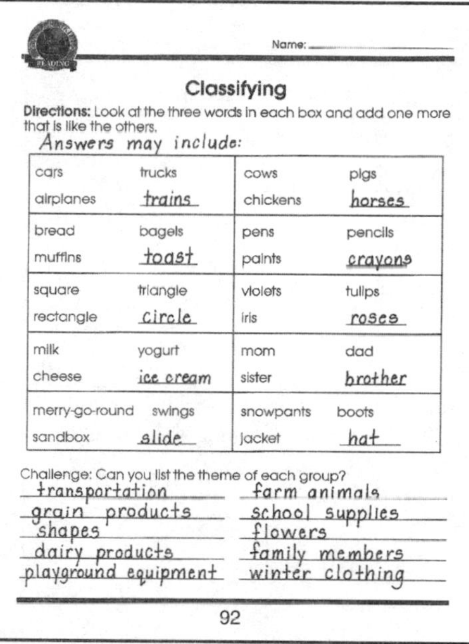

Name: ____________

Classifying

Directions: Look at the three words in each box and add one more that is like the others.

Answers may include:

cars	trucks	cows	pigs
airplanes	trains	chickens	horses
bread	bagels	pens	pencils
muffins	toast	paints	crayons
square	triangle	violets	tulips
rectangle	circle	iris	roses
milk	yogurt	mom	dad
cheese	ice cream	sister	brother
merry-go-round	swings	snowpants	boots
sandbox	slide	jacket	hat

Challenge: Can you list the theme of each group?

transportation — farm animals
grain products — school supplies
shapes — flowers
dairy products — family members
playground equipment — winter clothing

92

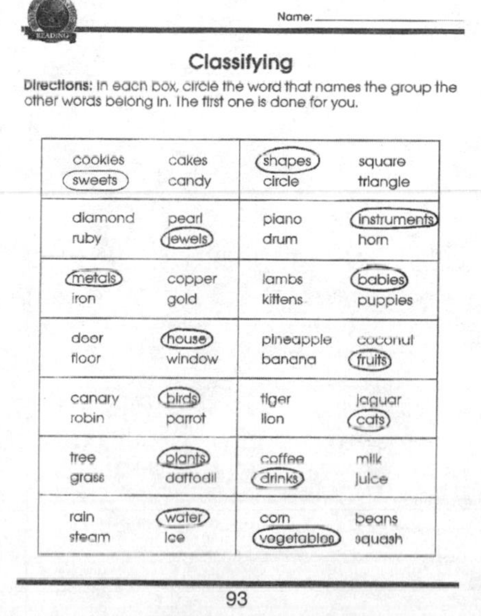

Name: ____________

Classifying

Directions: In each box, circle the word that names the group the other words belong in. The first one is done for you.

cookies	cakes	(shapes)	square
(sweets)	candy	circle	triangle
diamond	pearl	piano	(instruments)
ruby	(jewels)	drum	horn
(metals)	copper	lambs	(babies)
iron	gold	kittens	puppies
door	(house)	pineapple	coconut
floor	window	banana	(fruits)
canary	(birds)	tiger	jaguar
robin	parrot	lion	(cats)
tree	(plants)	coffee	milk
grass	daffodil	(drinks)	juice
rain	(water)	corn	beans
steam	ice	(vegetables)	squash

93

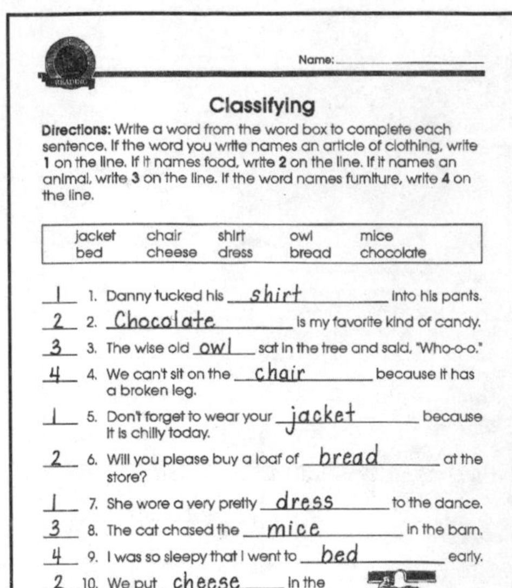

Name: ______

Classifying

Directions: Write a word from the word box to complete each sentence. If the word you write names an article of clothing, write **1** on the line. If it names food, write **2** on the line. If it names an animal, write **3** on the line. If the word names furniture, write **4** on the line.

jacket	chair	shirt	owl	mice
bed	cheese	dress	bread	chocolate

1 1. Danny tucked his shirt into his pants.
2 2. Chocolate is my favorite kind of candy.
3 3. The wise old owl sat in the tree and said, "Who-o-o."
4 4. We can't sit on the chair because it has a broken leg.
1 5. Don't forget to wear your jacket because it is chilly today.
2 6. Will you please buy a loaf of bread at the store?
1 7. She wore a very pretty dress to the dance.
3 8. The cat chased the mice in the barn.
4 9. I was so sleepy that I went to bed early.
2 10. We put cheese in the mouse trap to help catch the mice.

94

Name: ______

Classifying

Directions: Write a word from the word box that is described by the four words in each group.

cake	farm	sick	winter	kite	car
flower	dishes	puppy	storm	ocean	book

leaves petals stem roots flower	sand shells waves fish ocean	snow wind cold ice winter	string tail wind fly kite
fever headache pills sneeze sick	rain thunder wind hail storm	soft furry playful small puppy	sugar butter flour chocolate cake
tractor animals barn plow farm	cup plate bowl platter dishes	pages words pictures cover book	tires seats windows trunk car

95

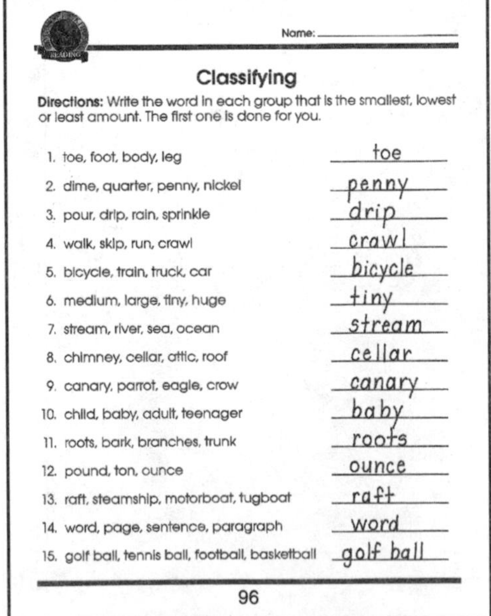

Name: ______

Classifying

Directions: Write the word in each group that is the smallest, lowest or least amount. The first one is done for you.

1. toe, foot, body, leg — toe
2. dime, quarter, penny, nickel — penny
3. pour, drip, rain, sprinkle — drip
4. walk, skip, run, crawl — crawl
5. bicycle, train, truck, car — bicycle
6. medium, large, tiny, huge — tiny
7. stream, river, sea, ocean — stream
8. chimney, cellar, attic, roof — cellar
9. canary, parrot, eagle, crow — canary
10. child, baby, adult, teenager — baby
11. roots, bark, branches, trunk — roots
12. pound, ton, ounce — ounce
13. raft, steamship, motorboat, tugboat — raft
14. word, page, sentence, paragraph — word
15. golf ball, tennis ball, football, basketball — golf ball

96

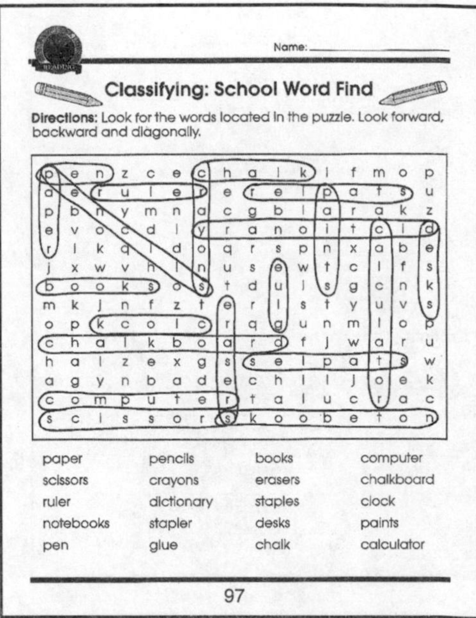

Name: ______

Classifying: School Word Find

Directions: Look for the words located in the puzzle. Look forward, backward and diagonally.

```
p e n z c e c h a l k l f m o p
a e r u l e r e r e l p a t s u
p b n y m n a c g b l a r a k z
e v o c d l y r a n o i t c l d
r l k q l d o q r s p n x a b e
j x w v h l n u s e w t c l f s
b o o k s o s t d u l s g c n k
m k j n f z t e r l s t y u v s
o p k c o l c r q g u n m l o p
c h a l k b o a r d f j w a r u
h a l z e x g s s e l p a t s w
a g y n b a d e c h l l j o e k
c o m p u t e r t a l u c r a c
s c i s s o r s k o o b e t o n
```

paper	pencils	books	computer
scissors	crayons	erasers	chalkboard
ruler	dictionary	staples	clock
notebooks	stapler	desks	paints
pen	glue	chalk	calculator

97

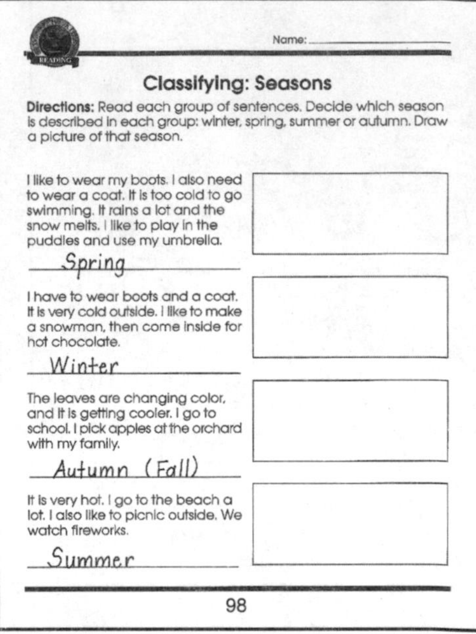

Name: ______

Classifying: Seasons

Directions: Read each group of sentences. Decide which season is described in each group: winter, spring, summer or autumn. Draw a picture of that season.

I like to wear my boots. I also need to wear a coat. It is too cold to go swimming. It rains a lot and the snow melts. I like to play in the puddles and use my umbrella.

Spring

I have to wear boots and a coat. It is very cold outside. I like to make a snowman, then come inside for hot chocolate.

Winter

The leaves are changing color, and it is getting cooler. I go to school. I pick apples at the orchard with my family.

Autumn (Fall)

It is very hot. I go to the beach a lot. I also like to picnic outside. We watch fireworks.

Summer

98

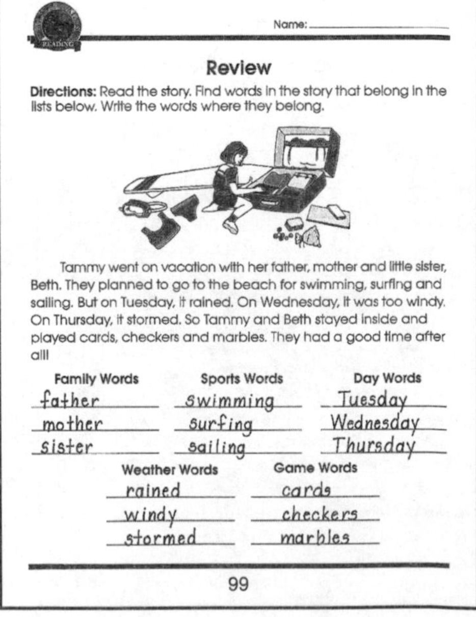

Name: ______

Review

Directions: Read the story. Find words in the story that belong in the lists below. Write the words where they belong.

Tammy went on vacation with her father, mother and little sister, Beth. They planned to go to the beach for swimming, surfing and sailing. But on Tuesday, it rained. On Wednesday, it was too windy. On Thursday, it stormed. So Tammy and Beth stayed inside and played cards, checkers and marbles. They had a good time after all!

Family Words	Sports Words	Day Words
father	swimming	Tuesday
mother	surfing	Wednesday
sister	sailing	Thursday

Weather Words	Game Words
rained	cards
windy	checkers
stormed	marbles

99

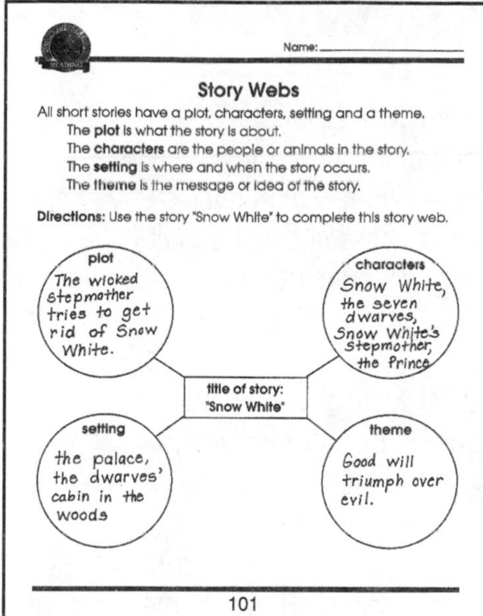

Name: ______________

Story Webs

All short stories have a plot, characters, setting and a theme.

The **plot** is what the story is about.

The **characters** are the people or animals in the story.

The **setting** is where and when the story occurs.

The **theme** is the message or idea of the story.

Directions: Use the story "Snow White" to complete this story web.

title of story: "Snow White"

plot: The wicked stepmother tries to get rid of Snow White.

characters: Snow White, the seven dwarves, Snow White's stepmother, the Prince

setting: the palace, the dwarves' cabin in the woods

theme: Good will triumph over evil.

101

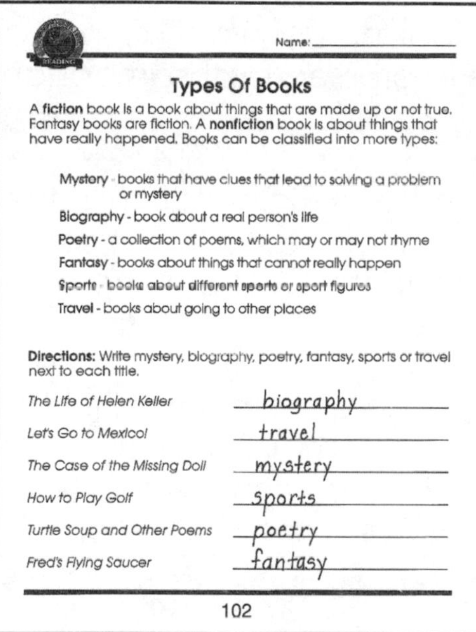

Name: ______________

Types Of Books

A **fiction** book is a book about things that are made up or not true. Fantasy books are fiction. A **nonfiction** book is about things that have really happened. Books can be classified into more types:

Mystery - books that have clues that lead to solving a problem or mystery

Biography - book about a real person's life

Poetry - a collection of poems, which may or may not rhyme

Fantasy - books about things that cannot really happen

Sports - books about different sports or sport figures

Travel - books about going to other places

Directions: Write mystery, biography, poetry, fantasy, sports or travel next to each title.

The Life of Helen Keller biography

Let's Go to Mexico! travel

The Case of the Missing Doll mystery

How to Play Golf sports

Turtle Soup and Other Poems poetry

Fred's Flying Saucer fantasy

102

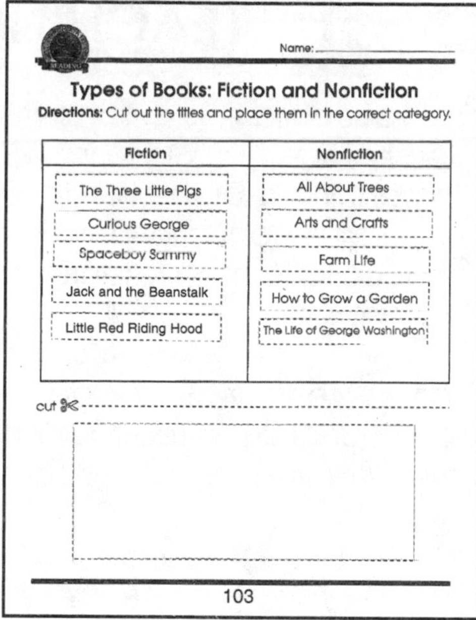

Name: ______________

Types of Books: Fiction and Nonfiction

Directions: Cut out the titles and place them in the correct category.

Fiction	Nonfiction
The Three Little Pigs	All About Trees
Curious George	Arts and Crafts
Spaceboy Sammy	Farm Life
Jack and the Beanstalk	How to Grow a Garden
Little Red Riding Hood	The Life of George Washington

cut

103

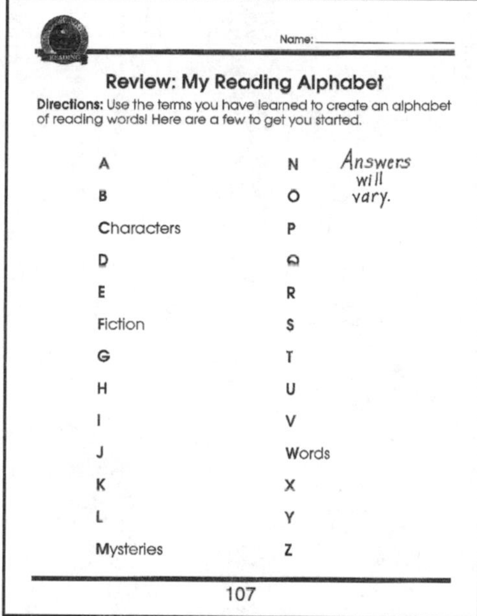

Name: ______________

Review: My Reading Alphabet

Directions: Use the terms you have learned to create an alphabet of reading words! Here are a few to get you started.

Answers will vary.

A	N
B	O
Characters	P
D	Q
E	R
Fiction	S
G	T
H	U
I	V
J	Words
K	X
L	Y
Mysteries	Z

107

TEACHING SUGGESTIONS

Make sure your child has a current library card and plan a special weekly time to visit the library together. On each visit, take a few moments to teach your child about different parts of the library. For example, on one visit, you can show him/her where fiction and nonfiction books are located. Regular library visits will help you to expose your child to many genres of books and help him/her to develop a life-long love of learning.

Read to and with your child, and let him/her see you reading for enjoyment. Encourage your child to read for enjoyment and make sure to provide many opportunities for your child to discuss what he/she is reading.

Ask your child: What if you couldn't read? Challenge him/her to make a list of as many kinds of reading as he/she thinks he/she does in a day. Then together keep track of every time you use reading throughout the day–reading directions on packages while cooking dinner, reading road signs, looking up information in a telephone book, reading mail, etc. Your child will be impressed by the important role reading plays in your lives!

When your child finishes a book, create fun ways to share the information in the book with you or with a friend. Some ways to do this might be to write a letter from one character to another, create a comic strip illustrating the events of the book or writing a journal entry one of the characters might write.

Encourage your child to dress up as a character from one of his/her favorite books and to act out events from the book for members of your family. Some fun characters to portray might be Winnie the Pooh, Ms. Frizzle from the Magic School Bus books, characters from Mother Goose rhymes, The Cat in the Hat, Amelia Bedelia and Cinderella.

Before you take your child to a movie or buy a new video, suggest that your child read the book first, or read it aloud to him/her. Talk with your child about the similarities and differences between the book and the movie and discuss which he/she likes better and why.

TEACHING SUGGESTIONS

Encourage your child to keep a "reading log" of books he/she has read, and write his/her reflections about each book. After your child has read several books, challenge him/her to go through the journal and classify the book titles by genre. Add symbols to indicate the types of books your child has read: F for fiction and N for nonfiction. To make this activity more challenging, further extend these classifications, indicating M for mystery, B for biography, P for poetry, etc. See page 128.

When you vacation with your child, purchase postcards from the various locations you visit. Let your child write important information about your trip on the postcards. Use a hole punch to make a hole in each postcard and fasten them together for a unique travel memory book!

Save the Sunday comics and cut out strips with interesting pictures or ones that tell a simple story. Cut the frames apart and challenge your child to re-order the story. Take this a step further by suggesting that your child create an extra frame to show what might happen next. For another activity, cut out or cover the text in the speech balloons and challenge your child to create a story that fits the pictures.

Check out a book on origami, the ancient art of Japanese paper-folding. Challenge your child to read the directions to create other figures from paper.

Reading Log

Book Type	Book Title	My Review of the Book

My Book Type Codes